THE
BARTENDER'S
GUIDE

This edition published by Parragon in 2008

Parragon
Queen Street House
4 Queen Street
Bath BA1 1HE
UK

ISBN: 978-1-4075-3397-1

Printed in China

Created and produced by Butler & Tanner Printers Ltd
Cover designed by Parragon

Additional text by Lisa Hughes and Sarah Johnstone

Contributing photographers: Mike Cooper, Charlie Richards, Günter Beer, and Carole McDonald. Special thanks to Beau Field and Raymond Law at Mu Mu's in Bristol, to Bibas in Bristol, and to Passvale Farm in Somerset for their help with location photography.

Additional photography: endpapers ©istockphoto.com/leadinglights; page 6 ©istockphoto.com/erichood; page 14 bottom right ©istockphoto.com/ifographer; page 15 ©istockphoto.com/nickfree; page 17 bottom ©istockphoto.com/dny59; page 18 top ©istockphoto. com/beans-, page 18 bottom ©istockphoto.com/ivanmateev; page 22 top middle ©istockphoto.com/sasodo; page 23 top right ©istockphoto.com/ dias46; page 25 ©istockphoto.com/2044photo; page 26 ©istockphoto. com/zonecreative, page 36 ©istockphoto.com/raatzie;page 42 ©istockphoto.com/luisportugal; page 46 ©istockphoto.com/muratkoc; page 52 ©istockphoto.com/chronistin; page 66 ©istockphoto.com/abzee; page 78 ©istockphoto.com/thedman; page 80 ©istockphoto.com/horst72, page 84 ©istockphoto.com/plainview.

Index by Nick Fawcett

WARNING
Recipes containing raw eggs are not suitable for the elderly, pregnant women, or anyone recovering from an illness.

Please drink alcohol responsibly.

THE
BARTENDER'S
GUIDE

Bath · New York · Singapore · Hong Kong · Cologne · Delhi · Melbourne

CONTENTS

FOREWORD
by ANGUS WINCHESTER

After nearly 70 years in the doldrums, the cocktail, and those that preside over its making and creation, is staging a resurgence. But, as with all things in the twenty-first century, it has become a more complicated affair. The humble but proud bartender has been replaced by the ingredient and technique savvy mixologist or even the bar chef. The few bottles and juices of the classic bar have been buried under a welcome avalanche of weird and wonderful liquors, fruit, and flavors from around the world. And no longer can the bartender, or amateur "shaker-upper," look merely to the United States for guidance and inspiration—the rest of the world has caught up quickly with fine drinks and bars aplenty.

But many of the basics from yesteryear still apply. A great cocktail is still a balanced potion of strong and weak, sweet and sour ingredients perfectly chilled and served in good glassware. A great bar, regardless of location, still combines excellence of service and ambiance, product and passion. And it is still possible to replicate the experience in your own home, as long as you remember that one cannot make a good product without good ingredients, a decent knowledge of technique, and a fine set of recipes to follow.

New drinks are created constantly, often with at least one eye on the classics that have gone before but with the other eye looking eagerly at the new liquids available. Some may be included in future books as fine as this one, others may only please those that were there at its birth, the recipe being only foggily remembered the next day. But the art of making drinks and the pleasure associated with it for all concerned will still be considered the most convivial of the culinary skills. And those that practice it, be they world renowned bar chefs or the home enthusiast, display a thirst for knowledge, a wonder at the array of flavors they have, and no small degree of obsessive compulsive behavior in their quest for excellence…and I for one am very glad for those traits.

Cheers…may the best of your past be the worst of your future.

Angus Winchester is a roving maven of drinks, dispensing fine cocktails and sage advice to drinkers and those that serve them around the world. He lives at 38,000 feet, has worked in several of the world's top bars, and has drunk in all of them.

INTRODUCTION

We've come a long way since the days when a cocktail meant a rather sickly, garish liquid, often premixed, with a paper umbrella balanced on the rim of the glass. Of course, if candy store colors and kitsch are what you like, each to their own, and there's nothing wrong with that, but elegance, sophistication, and indeed glamor is the modern fashion in cocktails.

This means that in the world of cocktails there is a renewed focus on fresh, high-quality ingredients, with sometimes subtle, sometimes startling, flavor combinations. Whether in a bar or at home, skillfully mixed drinks, carefully balanced to the specific taste of the person who's about to drink them, is the order of the day.

BECOME A GREAT BARTENDER

To be a great bartender you must combine the precision of a scientist with the creativity of an artist. A great bartender is both a technician and a chef; organized, efficient, and with a thorough understanding of the tools of the trade, yet sensitive, experimental, and with a flair for the theatrical. To be a great bartender you must be equally at home in the laboratory of your bar workspace, as well as performing on stage, attending to your guests' every need and presenting your creations with a dramatic flourish.

However, don't be put off. Becoming a great bartender is certainly an achievable goal, especially with this volume tucked beside your ice bucket. But remember that both substance and style are vital for great bartending.

Consequently, *The Bartender's Guide* inducts the reader into the mysteries of mixology; the science—and the secret—of the finest cocktails. In this section, aspiring bartenders can learn how to shake, stir, strain, and blend. There are instructions for constructing the perfect ice cube, and the complexities of layering, floating, and muddling are all made crystal clear.

The book also contains a range of other resources, including information on how to stock your own bar, a list of the tools of the bartender's trade, and a glossary of glasses. This explains how each glass got its name, when it should be used, as well as why it is important to use the right glass for a particular drink.

THE SOURCES OF SUCCESS

A good bartender has a real feel for the essential elements of a good cocktail, which is why *The Bartender's Guide* features a comprehensive lexicon of over 300 different drinks. From familiar spirits, wines, and beers through to more unusual liqueurs, flavorings, and nonalcoholic beverages. This section of the book groups together ingredients derived from the same raw materials and explains how they're made, how they're used, and how they're served.

It also offers some interesting insights into the history of many of the ingredients. These handy nuggets of often quirky information have been designed to catch the attention and they will help bartenders keep the conversational flow going while guests are waiting for their drinks to be mixed and poured.

A COMPENDIUM OF COCKTAILS

At the heart of this book are over 400 cocktail recipes. These are grouped by time of day or occasion on which you might enjoy them and each group is headed with a statement cocktail that epitomizes that particular moment.

From the traditional but mighty Martini to the new classic, the Cosmopolitan, via the Margarita, Daiquiri, and Caipirinha, all the famous names are here, but there is also a wide range of lesser known recipes that are due for a revival, as well as up-to-date and slightly unusual concoctions, featuring more obscure spirits and fresh fruits and herbs. The selection is broad and deep, and somewhere along this glorious spectrum you'll undoubtedly find a cocktail to fit any event or mood.

Each recipe has details of how many it serves and is accompanied by an icon that corresponds to the pictures in the glasses section so you can see which glass or glasses should be used for each cocktail. Many of the recipes also feature additional information and the story behind a particular cocktail.

This section also includes recipes

for a choice selection of delicious and refreshing nonalcoholic cocktails, often known by the jaunty soubriquet of "mocktails." So no one need feel left out—whether they're the designated driver, haven't yet reached the legal drinking age, or simply don't fancy drinking hard liquor.

BEST BAR NONE

And finally, to complement this wealth of practical and stimulating information, throughout the recipe section there are also features on some of the best bars in the world. There are ten in total, one from each of the world's top cities for drinking, each of which has its own unique and sometimes offbeat attractions.

From cosy snugs to cosmopolitan hangouts, from vertigo-inducing venues to sand-between-the-toes beach bars, these are places to visit should you be lucky enough to have the opportunity. If, on the other hand, you won't be traveling farther than your local liquor store this week, you can still soak up their ambience through this book and let their ethos inspire you.

Equally useful behind the counter of a neighborhood bar or on your coffee table at home, *The Bartender's Guide* is informative, educational, entertaining, and—like a great cocktail—a sheer delight. It's a one-stop shop for every aspiring bartender and adventurous drinker, so sit back, absorb, and enjoy. Then it's time to start shaking and stirring.

On a more somber and serious note, the purpose of this book is to encourage the enjoyment of fine cocktails and other drinks. The book is not intended to promote overconsumption of alcohol. When treated responsibly, alcohol is, of course, a pleasing mood enhancer, but inappropriate imbibing can lead to social and health problems, for individuals and for society at large. Consequently, the publishers of *The Bartender's Guide* advises readers to consume cocktails and any other alcoholic beverages wisely—so don't overdo it.

HOW TO USE THE RECIPES

At the heart of this bartender's guide are over 400 cocktail recipes. The recipes, which start on page 86, have been researched and collated from a wide range of sources. As a result, you'll find that most use measures, but a few use metric and/or American measurements.

Unfortunately there are no international standards for bar measures. A cocktail measure is usually approximately ¾ fl oz/ 1 tablespoon or 25 ml, which is where a jigger makes life a lot easier, although an accurate measuring cup is useful, too. This book gives cocktail recipes in American liquid measurements, including standard 8-ounce cup measures.

With the measures given in these recipes, it is essentially about the ratio of the base spirit to the modifier, the juice, champagne, or cream that holds the drink together and actually turns it into a cocktail.

As with any recipe, to get the required result you need to follow the instructions carefully. If the recipe says chill the glass, then chill it. If it tells you to fill the glass with ice, fill it. If it asks for cracked ice, don't use crushed ice. It's all in the detail, so don't be sloppy.

However, a good bartender will always fine-tune a cocktail and once you've mastered the basic recipe, try substituting one ingredient for a

similar one, adjusting the quantities slightly, or seeing what effect a different garnish will have. If you taste the resulting cocktails side by side it will help you develop your own palate and ultimately you'll be able to mix better drinks.

Where the recipe calls for ice other than ordinary ice cubes, then this is specified in the list of ingredients.

GARNISHES

From the classic cocktail cherry or olive through citrus slices, mini fruit kabobs, edible flowers, and kitschy accessories if you must, garnishes are part of the cocktail experience, and decorating a cocktail is part of the fun. Garnishes can even contribute to the flavor of a cocktail, particularly when it comes to lemon, orange, lime, and even grapefruit peel.

For a twist of peel, use a special citrus stripper, vegetable peeler, or small sharp knife. Try to remove as much of the white part as possible, and cut a piece of skin lengthwise. Twist this just above the surface of the drink, rind-side downward, to release the citrus oil, and either hang it on the glass or drop it in. To create a spiral, start at the top of the fruit and work your way around it.

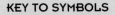

KEY TO SYMBOLS

☆ "Classic" cocktail

Y Cocktail or martini glass

▯ Highball glass

▯ Lowball glass

▯ Champagne flute

▯ Wine glass

▯ Shot glass

▯ Brandy snifter

▯ Sour glass

▯ Hurricane glass

▽ Coupette glass

▯ Pousse-café glass

▯ Irish coffee glass

▯ Mug or tankard

▯ Fresh pineapple

TOOLS
OF THE TRADE

What equipment you need in your bar or at home depends very much on whether you're the type of person who's determined to have all the latest gadgets and gizmo, or whether you're prepared to make do with what you've got. Either way, keep your bar area clean and tidy and your professionalism will undoubtedly impress your guests.

JIGGER

If you're making mixed cocktails, a jigger is essential, because it's the bartender's basic measuring tool. There are different styles, but the most common and useful type is made from metal and double-ended, with one cup holding approximately ¾ fl oz /25 ml/2.5 cl or one measure, and the other holding 1¾ fl oz /50 ml/5 cl or two measures. The cups may also be marked with lines every ⅓ fl oz / 10 ml/10 cl.

Optics aren't too expensive and they can make it easier to organize your space, but they are not essential.

SHAKER

The other essential for mixed cocktails is a shaker. Many professional bartenders prefer a Boston shaker, which consists of two cups, one of which can be used for measuring and stirring, which fit together tightly. The drawback to the Boston shaker, though, is that you need a separate strainer, such as a hawthorn strainer, which you hold over the top of the shaker as you pour.

Consequently, you may prefer to get a standard cocktail shaker, which also consists of two sections that fit together snugly, but which has a built-in strainer as well.

BAR SPOON

Of course, you can make do with a spoon from the kitchen, but a proper bar spoon has a small bowl and a long handle that allows you to muddle, mix, and stir with ease. However, you will have to raid the cutlery drawer for a teaspoon and a tablespoon, because you'll need these for measuring.

MUDDLER

For advanced mixing, particularly if you're mashing up citrus fruit or crushing herbs, you need a muddler. This is a chunky wooden tool with a straight shaft and a rounded end, which can also be employed to make cracked ice. However, if you don't have a muddler, you can also do the job with a mortar and pestle or a good old wooden spoon.

MIXING GLASS

Any vessel that holds about 1 pint of liquid can be used for mixing drinks in, especially if you're making several servings at once. A pitcher with a spout, to prevent the ice from slipping into the glass, is good, but not vital.

BLENDER

You'll find a blender with a pitcher very useful for making a wide range of cocktails, particularly fruit- and cream-based ones, especially if it has two speeds, so you can blend gently or vigorously. However, it is a good idea to get a powerful one that is also able to chop and crush ice in bulk, although manual ice crushers are available.

JUICER

A traditional ridged, half-lemon shape on a saucer will work perfectly well if you only require relatively small amounts of juice. There is also a gadget called a citrus spout, which screws into a lemon or lime and is useful for obtaining tiny quantities.

BOTTLE OPENER

A bottle opener is a simple, but efficient tool and you'll almost certainly have one of these already, although if you want to invest in a heavy-duty professional model that attaches to the wall or a counter top you'll be able to open bottles at top speed.

CORKSCREW

Again, there are many styles of corkscrews available, but whether it's a classic corkscrew with a metal spiral attached to a handle or a complex high-tech device that utilizes the principles of physics to the full, choose one that you know you can operate quickly and easily.

STOPPERS AND POURERS

A wine bottle stopper—the vacuum ones are good—and a champagne bottle stopper, which will keep the fizz in, are worth having. If you use a lot of cordials, you might like to buy a set of pourers, which fit into the top of the bottle and allow you to splash liquids into glasses with a certain panache.

CUTTING BOARD AND KNIFE

You'll need a small cutting board and a sharp knife for preparing fruit and garnishes. To pare orange or lemon peel, a specialty item of equipment called a citrus stripper is handy, but a vegetable peeler will do the same job, although with slightly less finesse.

ICE BUCKET

You can press pretty much any good-sized container into service as an ice bucket, but it's handy if it has a lid to slow down the melting process. Use tongs to pick up the cubes.

Of course, a ready supply of ice is vital for making cocktails and, if your bar is located some distance from the freezer you might consider investing in a small, portable ice-maker. However, ice is cheap to buy in bulk and a mini-refrigerator to keep some of your cocktail constituents cold might be a more sensible and economical purchase.

SWIZZLE STICKS

If style and sophistication is the effect you're endeavoring to create, paper parasols won't provide it, but if you're after a kitschy retro feel then swizzle sticks are the answer, particularly if you search out vintage ones, plus they can be used for gentle stirring and to stab wayward garnishes.

GLASSES

The bare minimum is wine glasses and tall glasses, but there are many different types of cocktail glasses, and many corresponding reasons for serving specific cocktails in them (see pages 16–19), so most bartenders will probably want to start their own collection.

THE BASIC INGREDIENTS

When you're stocking your bar you'll obviously need the ingredients for any specific cocktails you intend to make, and you'll want to buy any spirits that are particular favorites, but there are a number of items that any good bartender really should keep handy.

SPIRITS AND WINES

Gin
Vodka
Brandy
Rum
Tequila
Blended whiskey or whiskey
Dry vermouth
Sweet vermouth
Red wine
White wine
Champagne or sparkling wine
Malt liquor and/or beer

LIQUEURS

Triple sec, curaçao, Cointreau, or Grand Marnier
Blue curaçao
Kahlúa or other coffee liqueur
Pernod

MIXERS

Fruit juices (ideally freshly squeezed) and exotic juices
Sparkling mineral water
Club soda
Tonic water
Cola
Ginger ale
Soda pop (such as bitter lemon)

FLAVORINGS AND GARNISHES

Angostura bitters
Worcestershire sauce
Tabasco sauce
Grenadine
Superfine and powdered sugar
Sugar syrup (see recipe, right, to make your own) or corn syrup
Fruit syrups (according to preference)

Salt
Cocktail cherries
Cocktail olives
Cocktail onions
Lemons, limes, and oranges

SUGAR SYRUP

1 measure water
2 measures sugar

Bring the water to a boil in a saucepan. Remove from the heat and add the sugar, stirring until it has completely dissolved. Let cool, pour into a glass jar, seal, and refrigerate. The syrup will keep for up to one month in the refrigerator. Quantities can be scaled up or down as needed.

THE BARTENDER'S GUIDE TO
GLASSES

Some people would say that if you serve a cocktail in the wrong glass it's hardly worth bothering, so this guide will ensure you get it right.

COCKTAIL OR MARTINI GLASS

COUPETTE GLASS

CLASSIC GLASSWARE

A traditional cocktail glass is sometimes referred to as a martini glass, champagne glass, or stem cocktail glass. As with other stemware, the stem allows the drinker to hold the glass without affecting the temperature of the drink. The shape of the glass also helps keep the ingredients from separating, while the stem keeps the drink cool. Cocktail glasses are usually used to serve cocktails without ice. They vary in size and volume, but normally hold between ⅓ cup and ¾ cup. A variation of this glass is the double martini glass, taller and wider at the opening.

The most obviously recognizable cocktail glass, the conical martini glass, emerged with the Art Deco movement. It made its debut at the 1925 Paris Exposition of Decorative Arts as a clever twist on the goblet. And like most stemmed glasses—or "stemware"—this Y-shaped variety proved perfect for chilled cocktails, keeping people's hands from inadvertently warming their drinks. It gained popularity in Europe, particularly for Martinis, before proceeding to world domination after World War II.

Today's Margarita glass is based on the earlier champagne coupe, the saucer-shaped stem glass originally used for serving bubbly. Legend has it the coupe was modeled on a woman's breast. However, it was designed in 1663 so the story that it involved the anatomy of French queen Marie Antoinette must be apocryphal. To facilitate the rimming with salt necessary for Margaritas, the bowl of the coupette was widened. It's also used for Daiquiris.

CHAMPAGNE FLUTE

HIGHBALL GLASS

LOWBALL GLASS

The tall, thin flute glass has a hazy history. It dates back centuries, with its tapered design reducing the liquid's surface area and keeping champagne bubbling for longer. However, it only became fashionable in the 1950s, possibly after Austrian glassmaker Claus Josef Riedel began researching the way different glass shapes affect taste. Since then, flutes have largely supplanted the coupe for champagne and champagne cocktails— helped by the fact that more flutes fit on a serving tray.

Highball glasses are tall tumblers suitable for simple drinks with a high proportion of mixer to spirit. They're not only an essential component of any home bar, but the title "highball drinks" also encompasses a host of classic tipples, such as bourbon and water, scotch and soda, Bloody Marys, and Vodka Tonics. Highball glasses are versatile enough to substitute for the similarly shaped, but slightly larger, Collins glass. They're related to larger Zombie and smaller Delmonico glasses too.

The terms "lowball," "rocks," and "old-fashioned" are bandied around freely when referring to short, squat tumblers. As the second name suggests, they're perfect for holding ice and any spirit "on the rocks" should be served in one of these. Lowball glasses are also popular for short mixed drinks, such as Old-fashioneds. Variants include the Sazerac glass, named for the cognac-and-bitters New Orleans cocktail. The double rocks glass, nicknamed "the bucket," is used for tropical punch-style drinks

SHOT GLASS

BRANDY SNIFTER

SOUR GLASS

This is the home-bar essential that most frequently moonlights as a novelty collector's item. The regular, unadorned shot glass holds just enough liquid to be downed in a mouthful and boasts a thick base to withstand being slammed on the bar after the neat spirits or mixed-spirits "shooter" within has been consumed. Standard shot glasses are not just handy for toasts, they can stand in for jiggers too. And decorated with a variety of designs, they've become popular souvenirs.

The brandy snifter stands apart from other stemware. Whereas most stemmed glasses keep warm human hands off chilled drinks, the short-stemmed, bowl-shaped snifter invites you to cradle it in your palm, warming its amber spirit. The wide bottom creates a large surface from which the brandy can evaporate, and the aroma is trapped as the glass narrows to a constricted mouth, allowing you to inhale pleasurably before sipping. A snifter should be no more than a third filled.

As one of the oldest family of mixed drinks, dating back to Jerry Thomas's seminal recipe book *How to Mix Drinks* (1862), unsurprisingly sours have been served up in all manner of glasses, from lowball to martini. Sticklers for style, however, will be pleased to learn that standard drinkware exists. The glass specified for whiskey sours, pisco sours, and other citrus, sugar, and spirits drinks is a smaller, modified champagne flute—narrow at the stem and widening out at the lip.

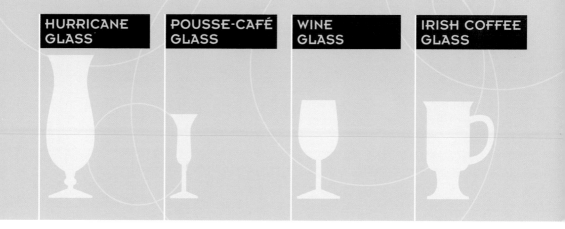

HURRICANE GLASS

POUSSE-CAFÉ GLASS

WINE GLASS

IRISH COFFEE GLASS

Most glasses are designed and named for certain drinks, but this isn't exclusively true of the large (26 fl oz) hurricane glass. Although originally badged to contain the passion-fruit-and-rum "Hurricane" cocktail at New Orleans bar Pat O'Brien's, its pear shape is a homage to the hurricane lamp. Today it's associated with frozen and blended cocktails. A frozen Piña Colada is virtually unthinkable without it, and it's often used for flamboyantly named cocktails of the Sex-on-the-Beach ilk.

These small, narrow-stemmed vessels have a modified hourglass figure, making it easier to create layered drinks in them. Essentially, they're cordial or liqueur glasses, with a flare at the top. Naturally, the art of any layered, rainbow drink is pouring the heaviest liqueur or syrup first and progressively layering lighter spirits. The bulb shape at the bottom, however, helps trap the lower layers and it's easy to gently drizzle liquids down the sides, thus causing less disturbance to those below.

White wine glasses tend to be smaller than red wine glasses, so use your judgment as to which will best accommodate the particular cocktail you are making. If a recipe mentions a goblet, however, go for a red wine glass or even a rounder balloon wine glass.

MUG

While not the height of sophistication, a mug is heatproof and is sometimes just what you need for a hot cocktail, especially if it's winter, the event is an outdoor one, and guests may be wearing gloves.

The key feature of an Irish coffee glass is that it's made of heatproof glass, which makes it suitable for hot cocktails such as toddies. It's usually short-stemmed, with a handle, or may have a metal base and handle.

TANKARD

Occasionally recipes call for a tankard—traditionally a large, robust, single-handled drinking vessel, commonly made of silver, pewter, or glass—but if you don't have one then a standard beer glass is a suitable substitute.

19

THE ART OF
MIXOLOGY

The secret of successful mixology lies in well-chosen spirits, freshly squeezed juices, just-crushed herbs, and—crucially—the skillful deployment of the tricks and techniques of the bartender's trade.

As with cooking and architecture, when it comes to mixing drinks, sometimes less really is more. Although expert bartenders always like to experiment with new and unusual ingredients, nothing beats a well-made classic. There are about half a dozen basic methods for combining cocktail ingredients, and it helps to know the pros and cons, as well as the best way of performing each.

BUILDING, LAYERING, AND FLOATING

Building a cocktail is the technical term for the simple task of pouring all the ingredients, one by one, over ice, into the glass in which the cocktail will be served. You might then stir them briefly.

Another important skill that the bartender must acquire is in the art of layering, which requires greater concentration, precision, and a steadier hand. To make layered shooters or pousse-café drinks, you generally pour the heaviest liquid first, working through to the lightest. However, the real trick is the technique. Either touch the top of the drink with a long-handled bar spoon and pour the liquid slowly over the back of it to disperse it across the top of the ingredients already in the glass. Or pour the liquid down the twisted stem that many professional bar spoons have. Hold the spoon's flat disk just above the drink. A little practice helps perfect both these relatively challenging methods. Floating is usually the term used to describe adding the top layer.

SHAKING

This is the most flamboyant method of making a cocktail—the one that James Bond prefers for his Martinis and that added some rocket fuel to Tom Cruise's career. Apart from so-called "flair bartending"—otherwise known as bragging—shaking is good for chilling drinks and diluting them to just the right degree.

First, the shaker should be filled to the three-quarter level with ice cubes. (Never use crushed ice because it melts and makes the drink watery.) The ingredients are then poured over the ice and shaken briskly for about 10 seconds, with the shaker gripped firmly in both hands.

The cocktail is sufficiently chilled and ready to pour when condensation appears on the outside of the shaker.

Strain the drink into a glass, leaving the ice behind in the shaker.

While it allows greater contact between cocktail and ice, and thus produces a colder drink than mere stirring, shaking also results in cloudier cocktails. It breaks tiny shards off the ice cubes, which then float in the liquid. The method also produces numerous tiny bubbles, which are great for some drinks such as Margaritas.

However, opinion over Martinis remains divided. Some connoisseurs claim that shaking the gin can "bruise" it and add bitterness. Others counter that shaking dissolves the vermouth better, leaving it less oily. Even formal scientific studies comparing shaken and stirred Martinis have failed to settle the debate, so it remains a matter of personal preference.

STIRRING

Stirring is the purist's choice, the mixology method that aims to retain the strength of the spirit. By carefully using a glass or metal rod (swizzle stick), or even a long-handled bar spoon, you can avoid chipping the ice cubes and making the cocktail watery. Crushed ice is an absolute no-no here. Drinks should be gently stirred in a mixing glass or the bottom half of a Boston shaker. As soon as condensation appears on the outside of the glass or shaker, the drink should be strained into a glass. Because the goal is a strong drink, some expert bartenders argue that those cocktails containing just spirits and liqueurs—in other words no fruit juices—should always be stirred.

CHILL THE "BURN"
Ice doesn't only chill cocktails, it mellows the "burn" effect of strong spirits and enhances their flavors, so always follow recipe recommendations precisely.

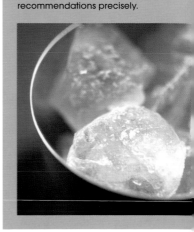

A TOUCH OF SPARKLE

To salt the rim of a glass, moisten the edge with a wedge of lime before turning the glass over and dipping it into a saucer of salt.

MUDDLING

In mixology, muddling isn't about confusion. Increasingly popular in bartending circles, it means to mash fruit or herbs to release their flavors and it's done with a wooden pestle-like implement called a muddler. The end used to crush ingredients is thicker and rounded; the opposite end, which is skinnier, is employed in stirring. Some also compare muddlers to rolling pins. The technique is to press down with a twisting action. Sometimes, a small amount of liquid will be added to facilitate muddling, but the majority of it is usually poured in later. Common muddled drinks include Caipirinhas (limes and sugar), Mojitos (mint leaves, sugar, and club soda) and Old-fashioneds (bitters and sugar syrup).

BLENDING

Electric blenders will mix ingredients that otherwise do not easily combine, so they are frequently employed when mixing alcohol with both fruit and fruit juice or alcohol with creamy ingredients. Strawberry Daiquiris and Piña Coladas are popular blended cocktails. As all the usual rules on ice are reversed in the blender and it's okay to use crushed ice, it's also used for so-called frozen cocktail versions, such as Frozen Margaritas. The cocktail should be blended until it's smooth, but be careful not to overdo it. The crushed ice should also be added sparingly.

ICE

Good ice makes for good cocktails, so use filtered or still mineral water with a low mineral content. Ordinary tap water contains all sorts of additives and, while they are harmless, they impart a flavor and will taint your ice.

If you want to make a very cold drink, fill the glass with ice, using large, solid lumps rather than small, fussy ones. However, bear in mind that as the ice melts it will start to dilute your drink, so drink up relatively quickly or the taste will be impaired.

If a recipe calls for cracked ice you can buy this by the bag or make it yourself, by filling a plastic bag with cubes, covering it with a towel, and then hitting it gently with a rolling pin. If you want crushed ice, then either buy it from a liquor store or specialty ice supplier—or bag the ice as before and hit it harder.

Ordinary ice cubes are cloudy. This haziness is partly due to the additives, but it's also caused by tiny fractures, formed when the water freezes. If you want to make clear cubes—and it's a classy touch—use filtered or still mineral water. Boil it to release any dissolved gases, cool it, and pour it into an ice-cube tray. As soon as the top of the cube has formed, puncture it. This will give the water inside a space to expand into, so it won't haze.

Once you've gone to the trouble of making good ice, don't ruin it by running the top of the tray under the faucet to release it. Either flex the tray carefully or run water onto the underside of the tray. Never handle ice. Always use tongs, so you don't transfer residues from your fingers.

BEST RESULTS

For best results, always chill your glasses beforehand by storing them in the refrigerator or placing them in the freezer for up to one hour before use.

THE BARTENDER'S
LEXICON
❖ OF COCKTAIL INGREDIENTS AND DRINKS ❖

Good bartenders are expected to be both gurus and geniuses. When it comes to what goes into a cocktail, they need to be the source of all knowledge, and, like an alchemist, they need to be able to turn those base elements into gold. To achieve this, good bartenders must have an intimate insight into the extensive range of cocktail ingredients, understanding the flavors and strengths of each one, what happens when they combine, and what will work in place of a particular element should it not be available.

The entries in this inventory are grouped by their major constituent or flavoring, so you'll find drinks distilled from grain, derived from sugar or flavored with citrus fruit together. Being able to offer an interesting tidbit or surprising fact as you serve a drink is also part of the bartender's act, and if you spend some time browsing this inventory that's exactly the kind of information you'll pick up. However, if there's something specific you want to find, use the index.

DRINKS DISTILLED FROM GRAIN

SCOTCH WHISKY

There are more than a hundred active distilleries in Scotland, located in six whisky-producing regions. Whisky has been made in Scotland since at least the fifteenth century, although its origins almost certainly go back several hundred years prior to that.

Scotch whisky is fermented grain that is distilled and then aged. The basic ingredients are spring water, malted barley, and yeast, but the unique variations in taste come from the precise attributes of the local water and other ingredients, the configuration of the stills at the distillery, the type of barrels used to age it, and so on. For example, once barley has germinated, peat fires are sometimes used to dry it and this can impart a smoky peatiness to the flavor of the malted barley. This will then be present in the taste of the whisky made from it.

There are basically two kinds of Scotch whisky—malt and grain. Malt whisky is only made from malted barley and is distilled in a pot still. Grain whisky is made from malted and unmalted barley, as well as other grains, usually wheat, and is distilled in a continuous still. Malt whisky from a single distiller is bottled in small volumes as a single malt or combined with grain spirit to create blended whisky. Scottish grain whisky largely goes into blends, although some producers bottle single grains.

In crude terms, single malts tend to be more expensive than blends, but this isn't necessarily a reflection of quality, as an individual might prefer the

An advertisement for Teacher's Scotch Whisky and Grand Liqueur in the 1901 edition of Scotland's Industrial Souvenir.

complexity and character of a particular blend and blending is an art in itself. For example, a blended Scotch whisky might be a mixture of as many as 50 individual malt and grain whiskies from a number of distilleries. Skillful mixing by the blender maintains the consistency and quality of the whisky. The age of the blend is the age of the youngest whisky in the mix.

Scotch whisky, which is spelled without the letter "e," must be made in Scotland, is generally double-distilled—although there are exceptions—and is matured for at least three years. Whiskey made elsewhere in the world, including North America, is spelt with the "e."

It's hard to give an ABV (alcohol by volume) for whisky or whiskey, but the standard is at least 40 percent. The classic way to drink most quality whiskeys is straight, with ice and or water to taste, although purists would say the taste is ruined by adding water. They would claim that if a drinker insists on diluting a Scotch whisky, they should do it with still Scottish mineral water, ideally the same water used to make that specific whisky, rather than chlorine-laden tap water, but that might prove tricky. Whiskies are also often mixed with club soda, ginger ale, or lemon-flavored soda pop, and are used in many cocktails.

SCOTCH WHISKY BRANDS

❖ **Glenfiddich** is a single-malt Scotch whisky produced in the Speyside region. The whisky is bottled at 12, 15, 18, 21, 30, 40, and 50 years old.

❖ **Glenlivet** is a single malt also produced in Speyside. The standard is the 12-year-old, aged in oak, that gives it a vanilla sweetness.

❖ **Glenmorangie** is a single malt produced in the Highlands. The water local to most Scottish distilleries is soft, but Glenmorangie's water rises through limestone and is hard, and this adds to its particular taste. As well as a ten-year-old and other vintage editions, Glenmorangie produces whisky with a sherry finish, which has been aged in old

sherry casks, a madeira finish, a burgundy finish, and so on.

❖ **Highland Park** is a single malt from Scotland's most northerly distillery, Kirkwall, in the Orkney Islands. The distillery still malts its own barley using Orkney peat which gives the whisky a heathery aroma. The standard bottling is a 12-year-old.

❖ **Lagavulin** is a single malt produced on the island of Islay, in the Western Isles, a short hop from Ireland. The 16-year-old is the standard and it has an ABV of 40 percent and a smoky, peaty flavor.

❖ **Laphroaig** is a single malt produced at a 200-year-old distillery, also on the isle of Islay, in 10-,15-, 30-, and even 40-year-old editions.

❖ **Talisker** is a single malt produced on the island of Skye, in the Inner Hebrides, using water from 14 underground springs. The ten-year-old has an ABV of 45.8 percent.

❖ **The Macallan** is a single malt from the Highlands. The company offers a wide range of whiskies of different ages, including a Macallan 1861 Replica, which gives the drinker a good sense of what a nineteenth-century-style malt would have tasted like.

Popular brands of blended Scotch whisky include Bell's, Chivas Regal, Johnnie Walker, Teacher's Highland Cream, and The Famous Grouse.

IRISH WHISKEY

In many ways, Irish whiskey is similar to Scotch whisky, but there are distinct differences in taste. For example, in Ireland barley is rarely malted over a peat fire, so Irish whiskey doesn't have the smokiness of Scotch.

The basic process for making Irish whiskey is much the same as that used to make Scotch whisky, but Irish whiskey tends to contain malted barley and a wider range of grains and it is usually triple-distilled in pot stills. Like Scotch whisky, it must be aged for at least three years. To be described as Irish whiskey, a spirit must also be distilled and matured in Ireland.

IRISH WHISKEY BRANDS

❖ **Bushmills** is a well-known brand of Irish whiskey. The company produces a 10-year-old and a 16-year-old malt, as well as the Black Bush blend.

❖ **Jameson** is another well-known brand of Irish whiskey. The blend is produced from 50 percent grain whiskey and 50 percent malt, aged in old bourbon casks for smoothness, with 10 percent in sherry casks for richness.

BOURBON

Bourbon is a whiskey that must be produced in the United States from a grain mash of not less than 51 percent corn and aged for at least two years in new barrels that have been charred inside. It is a sour mash whiskey, which means that a quantity of spent mash left over from the previous fermentation is added to each new batch of mash and yeast. The name bourbon comes from Bourbon County in Kentucky (ironically, the only dry county in the state), but the drink can be made anywhere in the county.

Well-known brands of bourbon include Jim Beam, with an ABV of 40 percent, Maker's Mark, which has an ABV of 45 percent or 50.5 percent in certain export markets, and Wild Turkey, which has an ABV of 50.5 percent.

RYE WHISKEY

Made mostly in North America, the basic process for making rye whiskey, or simply rye, is similar to that used

for making Scotch whisky and Irish whiskey. However, in the United States, rye whiskey must be produced from a grain mash made of at least 51 percent rye grain and aged in new barrels that have been charred inside. For Canadian rye, the only stipulation is that the beverage must be made in Canada. Rye whiskey is not usually as sweet as bourbon and the rye tends to give it a slight pepperiness.

TENNESSEE WHISKEY

Like bourbon, Tennessee whiskey is a sour mash whiskey, but it differs from bourbon in that it is filtered through maple charcoal before it is aged. There are no regulations governing exactly how Tennessee whiskey must be made.

The best-known brand, Jack Daniel's, is sold in distinctive rectangular bottles with a black label. It has an ABV of 40 percent. It is drunk straight, with ice, in mixed drinks, particularly with cola, and is an ingredient in several cocktails. Jack Daniel's is a brand with a loyal following. Frank Sinatra was allegedly buried with a flask of this whiskey by his side.

WHISKY/WHISKEY LIQUEURS

❖ **Drambuie** is a Scottish liqueur made from whisky flavored with heather, honey, and herbs.
❖ **Glayva**, another Scotch whisky-based liqueur, has similar flavors, but with the addition of citrus fruit.
❖ **Baileys Irish Cream** is an Irish whiskey liqueur containing cream—in fact, it is the original cream liqueur—with chocolate flavoring and an ABV of 15 percent. It is now also available with a hint of mint or a dash of caramel.
❖ **Sheridan's** is another Irish whiskey-based liqueur. It comes in a distinctive bottle that's divided into two sections, one containing a dark whiskey-based coffee liqueur, the other a creamy white liqueur. To serve, pour the dark liquid first and float the light one on top.

❖ **Irish Mist** is also a whiskey-based liqueur.
It is flavored with herbs and heather honey.
❖ **Southern Comfort** is an American whiskey-based
liqueur, flavored with, among other ingredients,
peach brandy, orange, vanilla, and cinnamon. It
is available in a range of different ABVs. It can
be mixed with club soda or cola and is used in a
number of cocktails.

HOME BREWS (MOONSHINE)

Irish home-brew spirit is called poteen. It is usually
distilled from grain or potatoes and has the highest ABV
of any drink in the world—according to legend at least.
Poteen, which is often rather rough, was banned in

Ireland for more than two centuries but was legalized in the late 1990s, although commercial versions tend to have a lower ABV than the bathtub variety. There are many variant spellings of poteen, including poitin, potheen, and potscheen. Private stills are illegal in most countries, partly because the government makes so much money by taxing legally distilled liquor and partly because of the possible danger to health.

VODKA

Popular all over the world, but with its origins in Russia (the Russians believe they invented it, but this is disputed), central, and eastern Europe (the Polish also claim they invented it) and Scandinavia, vodka is a clear spirit once used for medicinal purposes.

Vodka can be distilled from pretty much any plant matter that is sugar-rich and can be fermented, including potatoes, sugarbeet, and soy beans. Today, most commercial vodka is made from a mash of grains, such as wheat, rye, or corn, and filtered through charcoal. It has an ABV that ranges from 35 to 50 percent. Although it isn't usually aged, vodka is often flavored or sometimes colored with fruit, such as lemon or cranberry, or spices, such as pepper.

Vodka has the excellent attribute that you can't detect it on the drinker's breath and this neutrality makes it an important ingredient in many classic cocktails.

VODKA BRANDS

❖ **42 Below** is a 42 percent ABV vodka from New Zealand, available flavored with kiwi, passion fruit (granadilla), manuka honey, or feijoa.

❖ **Absolut Vodka** is a famous Swedish brand of vodka, distilled in Åhus in southern Sweden from local wheat grain and then filtered through charcoal. Absolut Blue has an ABV of 40 percent. Various flavors are available, including Citron (lemon), Kurant (black currant), and Peppar (jalapeños and green tomatoes).

❖ **Bison Grass** is a brand of Polish vodka. It's made in a style called zubrowka and flavored with a plant called bison grass—an alleged aphrodisiac—which gives it a yellow color. Every bottle contains a single blade of bison grass. Like other vodkas, Bison Grass is usually served chilled, but Poles mix it with apple juice, although outside Poland it's sometimes mixed with Red Bull for a double bovine hit.

❖ **Finlandia** is a 40 percent ABV brand of vodka made in Finland, available in several flavors, including cranberry and mango.

❖ **Grey Goose** You don't tend to think of the French as vodka makers, but this brand is produced in the Cognac region of France.

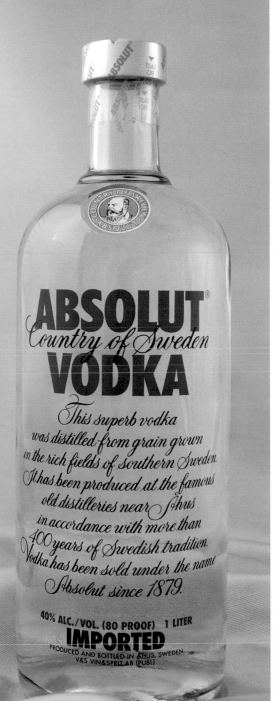

❖ **Reyka** is a small-batch Icelandic vodka filtered through lava rock at a distillery powered by geothermal steam.

❖ **Smirnoff** is a Russian vodka, claimed to be the first to be filtered through charcoal. It has several variants, including the premixed alcopop Smirnoff Ice, flavored with citrus.

❖ **Stolichnaya** is a Russian vodka made from winter wheat and Siberian glacial water, available in several flavors, including strawberry and raspberry. The Red Label version has an ABV of 40 percent.

❖ **Wyborowa** vodka is made in Poznan, Poland, using rye from the local area and water from an ancient local well.

GIN

This is a spirit distilled from any grain, potato, or beet, flavored with juniper and other herbs, and

usually redistilled. It originated in Holland in the seventeenth century, but quickly became popular in England and by the eighteenth century it was so cheap it was more widely consumed than beer, even though it was commonly flavored with turpentine. As a consequence, gin was blamed for a range of social ills—as illustrated by its British slang name, "mother's ruin"—and for London's high death rate at the time. In 1736 and 1751, the British government passed laws to tax gin sales and reduce consumption. Despite the odd riot, this was eventually achieved, although illicit gin stills continued to produce gin for the black market.

By the twentieth century, gin had managed to shake off its plebian roots and is now a spirit of some sophistication. It is usually drunk with ice and a slice of lemon. It is the base for numerous cocktails, including the classic Gin and Tonic and the Martini.

GIN TYPES AND BRANDS

❖ **London dry gin** was once produced in or near London, but is now just a dry gin with an ABV of around 40 percent. Well-known brands of London dry gin include Beefeater, Bombay Sapphire, Gilbey's, Gordon's—which holds the Royal Warrant for gin—and Tanqueray.

❖ **Hendrick's** is a brand of gin made in Scotland. It also has an ABV of 40 percent, but boasts an unusual additional flavoring in the form of cucumber—the maker suggests serving it with a slice of cucumber instead of lemon or lime.

❖ **Plymouth gin** is a brand of gin produced in Plymouth, Devon. The standard gin has an ABV of 41 percent, the Navy Strength version has an ABV of 57 percent.

❖ **Old Tom** is a sweetened American gin used primarily in cocktails.

❖ **Sloe gin** is a sweetened gin infused with sloes, the fruits of the blackthorn bush.

apple, pear, or plum, but unsweetened. This is a crucial difference between a schnapps and a liqueur. In Scandinavia, snaps or aquavit, usually distilled from grain or potatoes, possibly flavored but certainly not sweetened, is equivalent to schnapps. In all these places, schnapps is drunk straight, chilled, in small shots, during the course of a meal, sometimes accompanied by a fulsome toast.

Generally clear and somewhat similar in taste to vodka, schnappses have an ABV of around 40 percent or a little lower if they're fruity. However, they aren't drunk very much in the United States, although the peach-flavored Archers is one of the few widely available brands. Another, a Swiss schnapps called Goldschlager, is flavored with cinnamon and has little flakes of real gold floating in it.

Just to add to the confusion, a slang word for a liqueur in some parts of the county, is schapps, probably a relic from German- or Yiddish-speaking immigrants.

AQVAVIT

Aquavit (also known as Akvavit) is a clear or pale yellow Scandinavian spirit distilled from fermented grain or potatoes and flavored with cardamon, cumin, fennel, and especially caraway seeds. Aquavit is drunk straight and chilled, often with an appetizer of pickled or smoked fish, and has an ABV of around 40 percent. The name comes from the Latin for "water of life" (*aqua vitae*).

Around 15 types of akvavit are made in the Jutland town of Aalborg, the undisputed capital of the Danish akvavit industry.

Sloe gin is real easy to make at home. Pick your sloes from blackthorn hedges in October or November when they are ripest—probably after the first frosts. Take a liter (quart) bottle of gin, and drink half. Cut or prick the sloes and drop them into the half-empty bottle so that they displace the remaining gin to near the top. Add approximately 150 g/⅔ cup of sugar. All you have to do now is turn or agitate the bottle daily for a week, then weekly for a month or two, by which time it will be ready to drink (but it is best kept until the next winter).

SCHNAPPS

Something of a catchall term, in Germany, Austria, and Switzerland, schnapps (called *schnaps* or sometimes *korn* there) is a spirit or fruit brandy distilled from fermented grain or fruit, commonly

DRINKS DISTILLED FROM GRAPES

WINE

One of the most widely consumed drinks in the world, at its most simple, wine is just fermented grape juice. It arrived in Europe from the Middle East in around 5,000 BC. Wine is also an extensive and complicated topic, a subject that can take years to master. Modern wine-making is an extremely sophisticated procedure.

In essence, the crushed grapes (must) or pressed grapes (juice) are fermented for a couple of weeks. If the grapes don't contain enough of their own yeast for fermentation, cultured yeast is added. During this time the vast majority of the natural sugars turn into alcohol (ethanol). Then the remaining sugars are left to change into alcohol more slowly over a period of three to six months. Some wines are then bottled, while others are aged further in wooden casks.

Red wine is made from red or black grapes, but the color comes from the skins, which are left on during fermentation. White wine can be made from any color of grape, as long as the skins are separated and only the juice is used. Rosé is made by removing the dark grape skins in the middle of the fermentation process, or by blending red and white wines.

Wine can be described on a scale of dry through sweet, depending on how much natural sugar is left after the fermentation process. Even where one grape variety is dominant, most wines are blends of two or more varieties. Vintage wines are made from grapes that were all grown in a single year and are labeled with the date. Table wines normally contain between 10 percent and 14 percent ABV.

How a wine actually tastes depends on a range of factors, from the type of vine stock, the earth or *terroir* in which the vine grows, the weather in any one growing season, the choice of actual grapes, the fermentation process, how long and in what kind of container a wine is aged before it is bottled, and how long it is kept before being drunk.

The French are the premier winemakers and classic fine wines are traditionally from France, where wine production is controlled through a rigorous *Appellation* system—from *vin de table*, which must be French, through *vin de pays*, which has to be from a named region of France, through *Appellation d'Origine Contrôlée*, indicating wine from a specific district, produced according to strict rules. Italy, Spain, Portugal, and other European countries are notable wine producers. Wines from the United States, Australia, New Zealand, South Africa, Argentina, and Chile—known as "new world" wines—are now drunk around the globe.

Old world wines from Europe tend to be named for the area in which they were produced and the main grape variety. New world wines tend to be named for their predominant grape variety, although this is changing as the wine-growing area is seen to be increasingly important.

In general, white wines are served slightly chilled, while red wines are served at room temperature, but, of course, there are exceptions to these rules.

NATIONAL WINES

❖ **French** wine is often assumed—especially by the French—to be the finest in the world, but with the rise of new world wines from Australia, the United States, and South America, its position of pre-eminence has been threatened. The best French wines, however, are still the benchmark against which all other wines are judged and many French wine-producing regions are household names.

Bordeaux, for example, is a famous wine-growing region in southwest France, which produces the fine reds, Graves, Médoc, Pomerol, and Saint-Emilion, as well as the dessert wine, Sauternes. Claret is the name given to the red wines of Bordeaux, particularly those from the Medoc. Burgundy is another famous wine-growing region. It is situated south of Paris and includes the subregion of Chablis, which produces predominantly Chardonnay-based whites, and Beaujolais, known for its Gamay-based reds. Beaujolais Nouveau is the first bottling of the Beaujolais harvest, released annually to the public at midnight on the third Thursday in November—a time-honored marketing ploy. Burgundy's Côte de Nuits and Côte de Beaune produce some of the world's finest red wines, based on the difficult-to-cultivate, pinot noir grape.

❖ **Italian** wine is made in most regions of the country, because grapes grow just about everywhere in Italy, and there are many famous Italian wines, including Chianti, Barolo, and Valpolicella, all of which are red, and Soave, which is white. Wines based on the white Pinot Grigio grape are also made in several regions and are becoming increasingly popular internationally. Prosecco is a naturally fermented Italian white sparkling wine from Veneto, which takes its name from the Prosecco grape variety, while Asti (the Spumante has been dropped from its name), also naturally fermented, is a sweet sparkler from Piedmont that's often drunk with dessert.

The Italian system of wine classification and regulation has four categories, the top two of which are *Denominazione di Origine Controllata* and *Denominazione di Origine Controllata e Garantita.*

❖ **American** wines arre mainly produced in California, including the Cabernet Sauvignons of the Napa Valley and Sonoma, and the Pinot Noir of the Santa Ynez Valley, as popularized by the film *Sideways*, but other states, such as Oregon and Washington, are also increasingly important producers.

❖ **Spanish** wine is made in 50 recognized wine regions. Spain produces high-quality reds from Rioja and Ribera del Duero, fine whites from Rueda, and reds and whites from Penedes. Spanish sparkling wine is known as Cava and Spain also produces the famous fortified wine Sherry (Jerez). Its *Denominación de Origen* system classifies and regulates wine production.

❖ **Portuguese** wine includes some good table wines, particularly the reds from Douro in the north, all classified and regulated according to its *Denominação de Origem Controlada* system.

However, Portugal is best known for its fortified wines: port and madeira.

❖ **German** wine and the German wine industry were dominant in the nineteenth century, but their current reputation is for cheap and unchallenging sweet white wines—in other words Liebfraumilch. However, this is beginning to change and some of the country's smaller, and formerly great, producers are now endeavoring to produce high-quality, more imaginative wines, many of them based on the white Riesling grape. One of these is the unusual Eiswein, a sweet wine made from grapes left on the vine until the first frosts come—the word means "ice wine." Similar high-quality wines are also produced in Austria.

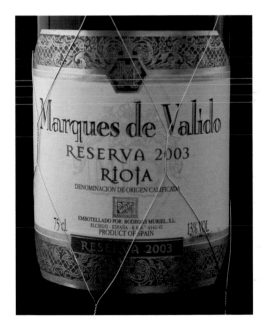

Some Spanish wines, particularly Riojas, come in bottles with a thin wire wrapped around them. This practice first became popular during the war to stop people from opening the bottles and replacing the wine with an inferior one. Today, it is more of a marketing exercise.

❖ **English** wine has a long history, and vines have been grown in England since Roman times, although the English wine industry consists of about 400 small vineyards with a correspondingly small output of principally white wine, the quality of some wines has greatly improved over the last few decades, and English wines are enjoyed and indeed celebrated in the United Kingdom. English wine should be distinguished from British wine, which is usually made from fortified, imported concentrates and is known to be cheap and of poor quality.

❖ **Australian** wines have become popular exports in the last couple of decades, but the country has been producing wine for more than 200 years and has several world-class wine-growing regions, predominantly in the southeast of the country, including the Barossa and Hunter Valleys, and Coonawarra. The reputation of "new world" Australian wines was founded on big, full-bodied reds from grape stocks such as Cabernet Sauvignon and Shiraz (Syrah in Europe), but today Australia grows most of the world's major grape varieties and most styles of wine are produced, including acclaimed sparkling wine and dessert wine.

❖ **New Zealand** wine has one really big name— the much-in-demand, intense, Cloudy Bay Sauvignon Blanc—but it also produces good white Chardonnays and Rieslings. The country's cool maritime climate also encourages the production of some fine red Pinot Noirs.

❖ **Argentinian** wine, the good stuff anyway, is mostly exported, while the not-so-good stuff is kept for home consumption. The country's own grape variety, Malbec, is used to make some of its strong reds. Torrontes, also specific to Argentina, is used for some of its whites.

❖ **Chilean** wine is an important export. The country's finest wines include those made with Carmenère, the country's own red grape variety.

❖ **South African** wine is traditionally white and based on the Chenin Blanc grape, but as the South African wine industry matures it is increasingly successful at creating good-quality reds. There are a number of wine-growing regions, but Stellenbosch is probably the best known.

CHAMPAGNE

Quite simply the most famous French wine-growing region in the world, Champagne specializes in wine that undergoes its second fermentation in the bottle. The result contains bubbles of carbon dioxide that give it that famous fizz.

When opening a bottle of champagne, aim for a soft pop, rather than a bang, as the cork comes out. The current fashion is for serving champagne in a flute, a delicate, tall, narrow glass, so the bubbles and aroma are retained. Tilt the glass slightly and pour the bubbly onto the side of the glass, until it's three-quarters full.

Well-known brands of champagne include Bollinger—abbreviated by its devotees to Bolly—Krug,

and Louis Roederer, producer of the luxury vintage champagne Cristal, famously guzzled by celebrities. There are also Moet & Chandon, whose brands include the luxury champagne Dom Perignon, only produced in years of exceptional vintage, Pol Roger, Taittinger, Veuve Clicquot, and Gosset.

Countries other than France produce fizzy or sparkling wines, but they're not allowed to call it champagne because the French have achieved legal protection of the name. In Spain, the equivalent is known as Cava, in Italy it's Asti, in Germany and Austria it's Sekt, and in the rest of France, outside the Champagne region, it's Crémant. Most sparkling wines are white, with Australia producing some sparkling reds and California well-known for its rosés. However, in less expensive products the sparkle may have been added by injection, rather than in-bottle fermentation.

SHERRY

In order to be allowed to be called sherry, this Spanish fortified wine must be produced in a triangular area formed by the three Andalucian towns of El Puerto de Santa Maria, Sanlucar de Barrameda, and Jerez de la Frontera—the word "sherry" is a corruption of "Jerez."

Versions of sherry have long been produced in the region. Because it is fortified, sherry tends to travel better than unfortified wine and it has been exported to the United Kingdom since the twelfth century. As a consequence, many of the sherry-making establishments, or "bodegas," were founded by British families in the late seventeenth and early eighteenth centuries.

To make sherry, wine is fortified with brandy and then, for a pale fino sherry, a yeast called *flor* is encouraged to grow on top to give flavor. Manzanilla is a light fino sherry that comes exclusively from Sanlucar de Barrameda.

Amontillado sherry is made in the same way, but after the flor has died, it is exposed to the air. This produces a slightly darker liquid. Oloroso sherry is oxidized for

United States, sherry is used as a generic term for fortified wine, but must be labeled with its state of origin, for example Californian sherry.

PORT

Made in the Douro River Valley in northern Portugal and exported through the nearby port of Porto, from whence it obviously gets its name, port is a red wine that is fortified by the addition of brandy, giving it an ABV of around 20 percent.

Port is especially popular in England, a tradition dating from the late seventeenth century and early eighteenth century, when England was at war with France. The English weren't able to get their hands on French wine, but the government reduced the import duty on Portuguese wine and it became inexpensive. On the long journey by sea from Portugal to England, however, the wine often spoiled, so the shippers began to add brandy to stabilize it and extend its shelf life. Eventually, instead of being added just before it was shipped, the brandy began to be added during the fermentation process—and port was created.

Port is traditionally an after-dinner drink and is often partnered with cheese, especially blue cheese. The best quality port is vintage port, made from the grapes of a single year's harvest, although not every year is deemed good enough to be declared a vintage. Vintage port tends to be unfiltered, so it needs to be decanted to remove the sediment before drinking, and should be served at room temperature.

Ruby port is a fruity, young, deep red port, a blend of wine from several different harvests that's usually aged for two or three years before bottling. Tawny port is either aged a lot longer than Ruby port, until it takes on a golden brown color and a more mellow, nutty taste, or it is made from lighter wines which give it a tawny appearance. Late Bottled Vintage, or LBV, is made from a single year's harvest and bottled after between four and six years aging. White port is made from white grapes, has a lighter, fresher

even longer, resulting in an even darker product. The variety known as medium sherry is usually sweetened Amontillado, while sweet sherry is sweetened Oloroso. Palo Cortado is a rare style of dry sherry, with a character halfway between an Amontillado and an Oloroso, produced when the flor or yeast fails to develop fully. Cream and pale cream sherries are usually blends of one or more of the three types of sherry, sweetened with dessert wine made from locally grown Pedro Ximenez or Moscatel grapes.

Sherry is drunk as an aperitif or sometimes as an after-dinner drink. It is essentially a white wine, so it should be served lightly chilled, although sweet dessert sherries are best at room temperature.

Well-known brands of sherry include the pale cream Croft Original, Harveys Bristol Cream, made from a mix of Fino, Amontillado, and Oloroso, sweetened with Pedro Ximenez, and the Fino, Tio Pepe. In the

taste, and isn't aged. It is usually drunk chilled, as an aperitif.

Port has many rituals associated with it. For example, in the olden days, at the end of a meal the ladies would retire and the gentlemen would pass a decanter of port around the table, but always to the person on the left of them. Anyone who kept the decanter in front of them for too long would be accused of being the Bishop of Norwich, a greedy cleric of yore. If you wanted someone to pass the port to you, you asked whether the person hogging it knew the Bishop of Norwich. If they misunderstood and said no, you would reply that he was an awfully nice man, but never passed the port.

Well-known brands of vintage port include Dow, Sandeman, and Taylor.

MADEIRA

Like its close cousin port, Madeira is a Portuguese fortified wine, although it isn't made on the mainland but on the island of Madeira, which lies out in the Atlantic, over 500 miles from the Portuguese capital, Lisbon.

Like port, Madeira is fortified with brandy, which was first added to help the wine survive long sea voyages, but unlike vintage port it is matured at high temperatures and oxidized, which gives it a more mellow taste and a golden brown color not dissimilar to that of tawny port.

Madeira should be served at room temperature, perhaps accompanied by a slice of Madeira cake, that doesn't contain wine, but which was invented in Britain specifically for this purpose.

wine is boiled in a still until the water and alcohol turn to vapor. The vapors are collected and condensed, so that they turn back into a liquid with a high alcohol content. The liquid is then aged, usually in oak barrels, and eventually diluted to between 40 and 60 percent ABV. The grading system refers to how long brandy is aged, in which VS (Very Special) indicates a product has been aged for at least three years, VSOP (Very Superior Old Pale) means five years, XO (Extra Old) is six years, and Hors D'age around ten years.

Brandy has been made in Armagnac for longer than it has been made in Cognac, and the wines used in both regions are largely from the same varieties of grape, but in Cognac the brandy is distilled twice, while in Armagnac it is almost always distilled just once. In exceptionally crude terms, this results in armagnac being more "gutsy" and cognac being more "refined" on the palate.

BRANDY

The name comes from the Dutch for burned (boiled) wine—*brandewijn*—and brandy is the word for a distilled wine. Distilled wines are produced in many countries, including Spain, Portugal, Germany, South Africa, and the United States, but "real" brandy comes from one of two *Appellation d'Origine Contrôlée* regions in France—Armagnac, in southwestern France in the foothills of the Pyrenees, and Cognac, in western France on the Atlantic coast.

Although the ancient Greeks and Romans distilled alcohol, brandy as it is drunk today first appeared in the twelfth century and became popular in Europe around the fourteenth century. Very simply, to make brandy,

Brandy generally has a caramel color, due to the effect of aging in wooden casks or, in less expensive examples, the addition of a caramel colorant.

Although essentially an after-dinner drink, when it is drunk straight, at room temperature, brandy is also a vital ingredient for many cocktails and indeed younger brandies are perfect for this purpose.

BRANDY BRANDS

❖ **Janneau** is a popular brand of armagnac, although the company has departed from tradition and uses a double-distillation process that was formerly the hallmark of rival cognac producers. Its range includes 5, 8, and 15-year-old brandies, as well as single vintages.

❖ **Courvoisier** is a popular brand of cognac. The Courvoisier company boasts a strong connection with Napoleons I and III, and produces a range of brandies. Courvoisier VSOP Exclusif, for example, is designed to be used as a mixer.

❖ **Hennessy** is another popular brand of cognac and the preferred tipple of many rap artists, certainly judging by the number of times it's mentioned in their lyrics. The product ranges from a standard VS through to an ultraexpensive Ellipse, of which only a hundred bottles are produced annually.

❖ **Hine Rare VSOP** is blended from more than 25 different cognacs, the youngest of which is at least four years old, as it must be to qualify for the VSOP designation. Hine Antique XO contains more than 40 cognacs, the youngest of which is at least six years old.

❖ **Martell VS** is a cognac blend that's aged for two years. At the other end of the company's range, Martell L'Or includes cognacs aged in barrels for more than 60 years.

❖ **Remy Martin VSOP** is aged in unusually small oak barrels that intensify the effects of the aging process.

OTHER BRANDY TYPES AND LIQUEURS

❖ **Marc** is a harsh French brandy distilled from the fermented pulp, skins, and stalks left behind after the grape juice is extracted for making wine.

❖ **Grappa,** the Italian version—made in roughly the same way—ranges from the eye-wateringly rough to a sophisticated spirit from a particular grape variety.

❖ **Aguardiente,** which translates as "burning water" or "firewater," is the generic Spanish name for a brandy with an ABV of between 30 and 45 percent. In Portugal, the same spirit is called aguardente. In Chile, aguardiente consists of distilled grape skins and pulp, similar to marc or grappa, but in Brazil, Colombia, and Mexico it's something different—a sugar cane spirit or rum.

❖ **Fruit brandy** is different again. This is the generic term for a brandy distilled from wine made from a fruit other than grapes.

❖ **Advocaat** is a Dutch liqueur made with egg yolks and sugar mixed with a brandy base and often flavored with vanilla. Advocaat is bright yellow and has a creamy consistency. Its ABV is usually between 15 and 20 percent and it is the principal ingredient in a Snowball. Famous advocaat makers include Bols and Warninks.

❖ **Alizé** At 16 percent ABV, this relatively low-alcohol liqueur is a blend of cognac, vodka, and fruit juice. It comes in Gold Passion (passion fruit), Red Passion (cranberry and peach), Wild Passion (pink grapefruit and mango), Bleu (cherry and ginger), and Rose (rose, strawberry, and lychee, but no cognac) versions.

VERMOUTH

Whatever variation you favor, vermouth is an essential ingredient of a Martini. A fortified wine with an ABV of between 15 and 18 percent, the red version was invented in eighteenth-century Italy by one Antonio

Benedetto Carpano, but the French developed a white version in the nineteenth century.

There are basically three types of vermouth. Red or rosso vermouth is sweet and is drunk straight as an aperitif or with a mixer. Bianco is, as you would expect, white and not as sweet as the red. Dry vermouth is also white and, well, dry. This is the one to use in a Martini. Although the red is sometimes known as Italian vermouth and the white as French vermouth, in practice all styles are now made by both Italian and French producers.

The name comes from the German *wermut*, meaning wormwood, which is one of the herbs used to flavor vermouth and which is indeed the crucial mind-altering component in absinthe. Vermouth contains only a tiny amount of wormwood, however, along with a range of other herbs and spices, the precise list depends on each producer's own secret recipe. The flavorings were originally used to disguise the taste of the cheap wine base. The fortification in today's commercial products is usually courtesy of a grape-based spirit.

Dry vermouth should be refrigerated and will keep for about six months. Other vermouths will last a year as long as they're stored in a cool place.

VERMOUTH BRANDS

❖ **Cinzano** is a brand of Italian vermouth, available as Cinzano Rosso, Cinzano Bianco, and Cinzano Extra Dry, as well as rosé, lemon, and orange versions. It has been made since 1757.

❖ **Dubonnet** is a well-known brand of French vermouth, flavored with quinine and bitter bark, and with an ABV of 17 percent.

❖ **Martini & Rossi** is probably the best-known brand of Italian vermouth. The name of the cocktail, in which vermouth is a vital ingredient, may not be named for the vermouth but may have other origins.

❖ **Noilly Prat** is a well-known brand of French vermouth, flavored with around 20 herbs and spices, and has an ABV of 17 percent.

DRINKS FLAVORED WITH HERBS AND SPICES

ANGOSTURA BITTERS

Angostura bitters is made from a secret blend of herbs and spices and is best described as a concentrated flavoring. Despite its name, the theory is that it isn't bitter when added to a drink, but has the ability to bring out the flavor of the other ingredients. It was invented in the nineteenth century by an army doctor in Venezuela, who used it to improve the appetite of his soldiers, but it is now made in Trinidad. It has a high ABV of 44.7 percent, but rarely more than a couple of splashes are added to mixed drinks. Angostura has a distinctive label that's too big for the bottle—apparently an error that nobody got around to rectifying. It is the "pink" in a Pink Gin—simply gin and Angostura bitters.

PIMM'S

Pimm's was invented in the early nineteenth century by James Pimm, the proprietor of a City of London oyster bar. Pimm's No. 1 Cup is a fruity, gin-based drink flavored with a secret mix of herbs. Although originally sold as an aid to digestion, Pimm's, the color of strong tea with a pinky blush, is a quintessentially English summer drink.

The traditional way to serve Pimm's No. 1 is to mix up a pitcher of one part Pimm's to two parts lemon-flavored soda pop and add a veritable fruit cocktail of orange, lemon, apple, and cucumber slices, plus a few sprigs of mint and ice. Pimm's is also used as an ingredient in a range of other cocktail recipes.

At one time, a range of Pimm's concoctions existed, numbered one through six, each based on a different

The recipe for Angostura bitters was developed in 1824 by Dr. Johann Gottlieb Benjamin Siegert, a surgeon in Simon Bolívar's army. He was based in Ciudad Bolívar in Venezuela, which was then known as Angostura, and used locally available ingredients.

By the late nineteenth century, absinthe had become associated with Parisian artists and writers, but it was also thought to be dangerously addictive and was blamed for a variety of social ills, including violent crime. Consequently, in 1915, it was banned in France. However, by the late twentieth century the European Union relaxed the ban and absinthe has since enjoyed a revival. It remains illegal to produce and sell, although not to consume, absinthe in the United States.

The classic way to prepare absinthe is to place a sugar cube on a spoon over a glass, then pour a slug of absinthe over the sugar cube and set light to it. When the sugar has melted and dripped into the glass, add ice-cold water (three to five parts to one part absinthe) to douse the flames and to taste. Diluting absinthe causes it to go cloudy. This is known as "louching," from the French word for a ladle.

spirit, but these were dropped in the 1970s and in addition to No. 1, the only other Pimm's now available is the No. 3, which carries the sobriquet Winter, is based on brandy, and has a spicier, more orangey taste. Both Pimm's No. 1 and No. 3 have an ABV of 25 percent.

ABSINTHE

Absinthe derives its name from the Latin for wormwood (*Artemesia absinthium*). The spirit is distilled from a mixture of bitter herbs, including wormwood, aniseed, angelica, and cloves. Legend has it that a Frenchman called Dr. Ordinaire invented absinthe as a patent medicine sometime in the late eighteenth century. Its greeny yellowish color—and some would say its taste— are certainly somewhat medicinal, but it is a highly alcoholic spirit, which can range from 50 to 90 percent ABV, and its effects are far more likely to be detrimental than beneficial to the drinker's health.

Also known as "green fairy" and "la fée," in Italy absinthe is called assenzio, in Spain it's ajenjo, and in Morocco it's chiba. Such is the mystique surrounding absinthe that various specialized items of equipment are associated with it, including slotted absinthe spoons.

LILLET

Lillet is a French fortified wine, available in red and white, and flavored with herbs and fruits.

MEAD

Mead consists of fermented honey and water often flavored with a few herbs. It's always cited as the oldest alcoholic drink known to humankind.

TABASCO

Tabasco is a hot pepper sauce made in Louisiana from tabasco peppers and other ingredients. It's often used to put a kick into a Bloody Mary.

WORCESTERSHIRE SAUCE

Worcestershire sauce is a fermented spicy sauce containing, among other ingredients, vinegar, molasses, and anchovies. It is often used to liven up a Bloody Mary, too. The most famous brand is Lee & Perrins.

LIQUEURS FLAVORED WITH HERBS AND SPICES

❖ **Chartreuse** is a French liqueur flavored with herbs and originally made by monks. As with many of the ancient herb liqueurs, the exact recipe is top secret and allegedly only the three monks who prepare the herbal mixture are in possession of it.

Green chartreuse is bright green and has an ABV of 55 percent, while yellow chartreuse has an ABV of 40 percent and is sweeter. The yellowish green color chartreuse is named for the drink.

❖ **Benedictine** was developed in the sixteenth century by a Benedictine monk called Dom Bernardo Vincelli at an abbey in Normandy, France. It is a cognac-based liqueur flavored with herbs. The exact recipe is a closely guarded secret and it's said that only three people know it at any one time. The company that owns the Benedictine brand also produces a liqueur called B and B, in which Benedictine is further diluted with brandy to make it drier.

Tabasco sauce is made from tabasco peppers, vinegar, and salt, and aged in white oak barrels for three years. The peppers are grown on Avery Island in Louisiana, as well as in Central and South America, and are handpicked to ensure they are ripe. Tabasco, a registered brand name, has been produced by the McIlhenny Company since 1868.

❖ **Angelica** is a pale yellow French liqueur, 40 percent ABV, flavored with angelica and made in the Pyrenees region. There is also a yellow Spanish liqueur of the same name.

❖ **Crème de Noyaux** is a French, almond-flavored liqueur that is white or pink in color.

❖ **Parfait Amour** is a purple liqueur, made in France and Holland, which usually has a curaçao base, flavored with vanilla, almonds, and rose petals.

❖ **Cuarenta Y Tres** is another yellow liqueur from Spain, flavored with forty-three fruits and herbs, hence the name, which is Spanish for 43. It's also known as Licor 43.

❖ **Amaretto** is a golden brown Italian liqueur with a bitter-sweet almond taste. Disaronno Originale is a well-known brand of amaretto. It has an ABV of 28 percent and is flavored with burned sugar, and 17 herbs and fruits soaked in apricot kernel oil. Disaronno is made in the Italian town of Saronno, near Lake Como, traces its history back to 1525, and comes in a distinctive square bottle. Amaretto di Amore is another well-known brand of amaretto.

❖ **Fernet Branca and Strega** are Italian herbal liqueurs, made from more than 40 herbs and spices, drunk straight as a digestif, or mixed with coffee or cola. They have an ABV of 40 percent. A mint-flavored version of Fernet Branca, called Branca Menta, is also available. Strega is flavored with violets and herbs, including mint and saffron, which gives it a yellow color. Isolabella is yet another Italian liqueur flavored with herbs, while Frangelico, also from Italy, gets its flavor from herbs and hazelnuts.

❖ **Campari** is an Italian liqueur with an ABV of 25 percent, invented in the nineteenth century by one Gaspare Campari. As ever, its exact composition is shrouded in mystery, but it contains a bitter-sweet mix of around 60 herbs and spices, although sources differ as to what gives it its distinctive red color—it could be cochineal or capsicum. Either way, campari is traditionally served as an aperitif, straight or with club soda.

❖ **Kümmel** is a clear German, Dutch, sometimes Russian, or even Danish liqueur, flavored with caraway. It is also known as kimmel. Underberg is a bitter, German digestif, sold in small, single-glass bottles with a distinctive paper wrapper, while Danziger Goldwasser is another German liqueur flavored with herbs, but distinguished by the small specks of genuine gold floating in it.

❖ **Swedish Punsch** is a Swedish liqueur based on arak and flavored with various spices, lemon, and sugar.

❖ **Metaxa** is a Greek liqueur made of blended brandy and wine flavored with herbs.

❖ **Pisang Ambon** is a bright green fruit-and-herb liqueur with a strong taste of banana, which originated in southeast Asia and is now produced by Dutch company, Lucas Bols.

GINGER-FLAVORED DRINKS

❖ **Ginger beer**'s origins stretch back to the eighteenth century and cloudy ginger beer is a quintessentially English summer drink. Mildly fizzy and gently alcoholic, its basic ingredients are ginger, lemon, sugar, and a fermenting agent, traditionally a yeast-and-bacteria combination known as "the ginger beer plant," but any other yeast can be used. Nowadays, ginger beer sold commercially is usually nonalcoholic and more akin to ginger ale, a soda pop flavored with ginger.

❖ **Ginger wine** is a grape-based wine flavored with ginger and other spices. One of the best-known brands is Stone's Original Green Ginger Wine, very popular in Britain and made since the eighteenth century. Ginger wine experienced a particularly

Native to South-East Asia, ginger has long been prized for its aromatic, culinary and medicinal properties. In an attempt to make it more available, Spanish explorers introduced ginger to the West Indies, Mexico and South America in the sixteenth century, and these areas began exporting the precious herb back to Europe. Today, the top commercial producers of ginger include Jamaica, India, Fiji, Indonesia and Australia.

strong sales boost during the cholera epidemic of the 1830s, because ginger was believed to offer protection against the disease. It is a 13 percent ABV fortified grape wine with added ground ginger and raisins. As well as being drunk straight, it is traditionally splashed into whiskey to create a Whiskey Mac. There is also a Special Reserve version with an ABV of 18 percent. Crabbie's Green Ginger Wine is another well-known brand.

❖ **Falernum** is a sweet, thick, clear syrup used in Caribbean drinks, which contains, among other flavorings, ginger, cloves, lime, and sometimes vanilla or allspice. It can be alcoholic or nonalcoholic.

HERB-FLAVORED SODAS

❖ **Cola** is a nonalcoholic, carbonated drink, brown in color and flavored with citrus fruit and spices. In common with most soft drinks, cola is drunk on its own, chilled or with ice, but it also mixes well with spirits such as rum or some types of whiskey. Well-known brands include Coca-Cola and Pepsi Cola.

❖ **Root beer** is a popular nonalcoholic drink originally made from sassafrass leaves and roots. It is now flavored with other roots, berries, barks, plant materials, and herbs. Birch beer is another nonalcoholic drink, available in the Philadelphia region. Alcoholic root beers are also available in the United States.

❖ **Dr. Pepper** is a well-known brand of nonalcoholic carbonated drink, made to a secret formula of 23 ingredients, but tasting of cherries and colored with caramel.

DRINKS FLAVORED WITH ANISEED

PASTIS

Pastis is an aniseed-flavored liqueur or anisette, drunk widely in France, often as an aperitif. Typically it contains 40 to 45 percent ABV. In 1915, absinthe was banned in France. Facing ruin, absinthe producers reengineered their potent spirit, removing the wormwood, adding more aniseed, and reducing the alcohol content to create pastis. Normally diluted with five parts water, customers like to mix their own, so it is usually served with a pitcher of iced water. Well-known brands of pastis include Pernod, Ricard, and Pastis 51.

RAKI

Raki is often described as the national drink of Turkey, but it is also made in the Balkans and Middle East. Recipes vary, but raki is distilled, generally flavored with aniseed, and tends to be drunk chilled and diluted as an aperitif, perhaps with a plate of meze or hors d'oeuvres. Raki is also known as arak or lion's milk.

SAMBUCA

Sambuca is a clear Italian liqueur flavored with aniseed. It can be drunk straight or with ice and is sometimes served with three coffee beans, floating in it, to represent health, wealth, and happiness.

GALLIANO

Galliano is a bright yellow Italian liqueur, often used in a Harvey Wallbanger and in Long Island Iced Tea.

JÄGERMEISTER

Jägermeister is a dark red German liqueur flavored with herbs, including aniseed, and drunk as a digestif.

OUZO

Ouzo is a clear Greek liqueur flavored with aniseed. It can be drunk straight or with water.

DRINKS MADE FROM CITRUS FRUIT

TRIPLE SEC

Triple sec is a colorless orange-flavored distilled liqueur used in numerous cocktails as a sweetener, with an ABV of between 15 and 40 percent.

CURAÇAO

Curaçao is a clear (or white) bitter orange liqueur. It was originally made on the Caribbean island of Curaçao from the bitter peel of the laraha orange, but is now produced in numerous countries and colors, notably green, red, purple, and blue, the last tending to be the most popular. These exotic hues are achieved by the addition of artificial coloring, but make curaçao extremely useful for cocktails.

GRAND MARNIER

Grand Marnier is a French orange liqueur blended from cognac and a type of triple sec or curaçao derived from aromatic bitter oranges. The Cordon Rouge or red ribbon variety is the original and has an ABV of 40 percent, while the Cordon Jaune or yellow ribbon is of lesser quality. Grand Marnier can be drunk straight, over ice, or used in cocktails.

COINTREAU

Cointreau is also a clear orange liqueur made from dried bitter orange peel and sweet orange peel in Angers, France. It has an ABV of 40 percent and is commonly served as both an aperitif and a digestif, but is also used in cocktails.

AURUM

Aurum is a golden, orange-flavored Italian liqueur with an ABV of 40 percent. Tuaca is a brandy-based liqueur from Italy, flavored with vanilla and orange.

LIMONCELLO

Limoncello is a sweet, lemony liqueur from southern Italy. It is not sour, because it is made from lemon peel rather than juice, combined with a range of alcoholic bases. It is usually chilled and served as an after-dinner drink, but also appears in cocktails.

LEMON-FLAVORED SOFT DRINKS

Lemonade is a nonalcoholic lemon-flavored drink made of water, sugar, and lemon juice. When commercially produced as a soda pop, such as 7-Up or Sprite, it is usually clear, effervescent, and containing both lemon and lime flavoring. This is in contrast to homemade or traditional lemonade, which is cloudy and is not carbonated. As well as being drunk on its own, chilled or with ice, these beverages mix well and are added to many cocktails. Bitter lemon—tonic water with added lemon flavoring—is also frequently used as a mixer. Hooper's Hooch is an alcoholic bottled lemonade with an ABV of 4.7 percent—what is often called an "alcopop." Like many lemon- and orange-based drinks, it is also available in other fruit flavors.

FRUIT JUICE

Fruit juice is both the unadulterated juice extracted from any fruit, obviously not just citrus fruit, or a drink made from extract or concentrate, sugar, and water.

BELVOIR

Belvoir is a brand of nonalcoholic, fruit-based, traditionally styled cordials and pressés (a mix of fruit juice and sparkling mineral water), some of which are organic.

ORANGE BITTERS

Orange bitters is a cocktail flavoring not unlike Angostura bitters, but usually made from the peel of unripe oranges.

DRINKS MADE FROM SOFT OR EXOTIC FRUIT

FRUIT BRANDY

Fruit brandy is the generic term for a brandy distilled from wine made from a fruit other than grapes, as opposed to fruit-flavored brandy, which is grape wine brandy flavored with another fruit. Fruit brandy is made all over the world, from a range of fruits, including cherries, apricots, and peaches.

KIRSCHWASSER

Kirschwasser is a German fruit brandy made from black cherries, with an ABV of around 40 percent. Kirschwasser is frequently abbreviated to kirsch. It is drunk alone or in cocktails, and is also used to flavor cheese fondue and a variety of cakes and desserts.

CHERRY HEERING

Cherry Heering is a well-known brandy-based liqueur flavored with cherries, produced by the Danish company Peter Heering.

MIRABELLE

Mirabelle is a French fruit brandy made from plums, with an ABV of around 40 percent.

QUETSCH

Quetsch is a German fruit brandy distilled from fermented plums, with an ABV of around 40 percent.

Fruits with soft flesh, such as cherries, have been served in alcohol since Roman times. The alcohol was first used to preserve the fruits. The full flavor of cherries also complement the acidity of the alcohol and add to its taste.

SLIVOVITZ

Slivovitz is an Eastern European and Balkan fruit brandy made from plum wine, with an ABV of around 40 percent.

PALINKA

Palinka is a Hungarian fruit brandy, usually made from plum wine, but also from other soft fruit wine, with an ABV of around 40 percent.

LIQUEURS FLAVORED WITH SOFT OR TROPICAL FRUITS

It's difficult to give a precise definition of the word liqueur, but generally it means a spirit that is flavored with fruit, herbs, or spices and sweetened, although it can also mean a distilled fruit wine. Liqueurs are now made all over the world (in the United States they are also known as cordials). Their origins can be traced back to the herbal medicines made by medieval monks.

Although often an after-dinner drink, there are no hard and fast rules about when to serve liqueurs, and they can be consumed straight, with ice, or in coffee. They are also an important ingredient in a wide range of cocktails. Many cocktail recipes mix a liqueur with cream, and cream liqueurs, such as Baileys Irish Cream, are now sold premixed. Crème liqueurs, on the other hand, tend not to contain real cream and are usually very syrupy liqueurs that have been particularly heavily sweetened. Liqueurs can have an ABV of between 15 and 30 percent, but some can be as potent as 55 percent ABV.

❖ **Maraschino** is a clear cherry liqueur, made from maraska cherries and their crushed kernels. It has an ABV of around 30 percent.

❖ **Abricotine** is a yellow apricot liqueur from France with an ABV of 31.5 percent. It's strong almond flavor is due to the inclusion of the apricot kernels.
❖ **Midori** is a melon liqueur. It's bright green in color and has an ABV of 30 percent.
❖ **Amarula Cream** is a 17 percent ABV South African liqueur distilled from wine made from the fruit of the marula or elephant tree and mixed with cream.

❖ **Kibowi** is a liqueur made in Holland, flavored with kiwi.

❖ **Crème de cassis** is a black currant-flavored liqueur, most commonly used in the cocktails Kir (crème de cassis and white wine) and Kir Royale (crème de cassis and champagne).

❖ **Framboise** is the name given to a raspberry-flavored liqueur, a clear, raspberry-flavored brandy, and a Belgian raspberry fruit beer.

❖ **Grenadine** is not actually a liqueur, because it is nonalcoholic. It is a red, pomegranate-flavored syrup used to color and sweeten cocktails. A green version is also available.

Lapponia Lakka is a Finnish liqueur made from cloudberries. Cloudberries are golden-colored and closely related to the raspberry. They grow in the cold northern climates of Scandinavia, Scotland, Siberia, and Canada, as well as the Arctic Circle. They are one of the most delicious and costly of all berries because of their limited growing area. Because they grow in cold temperatures, the berries ripen slowly, allowing the flavor to develop to an extraordinary intensity and sweetness, tasting almost like honeyed apples.

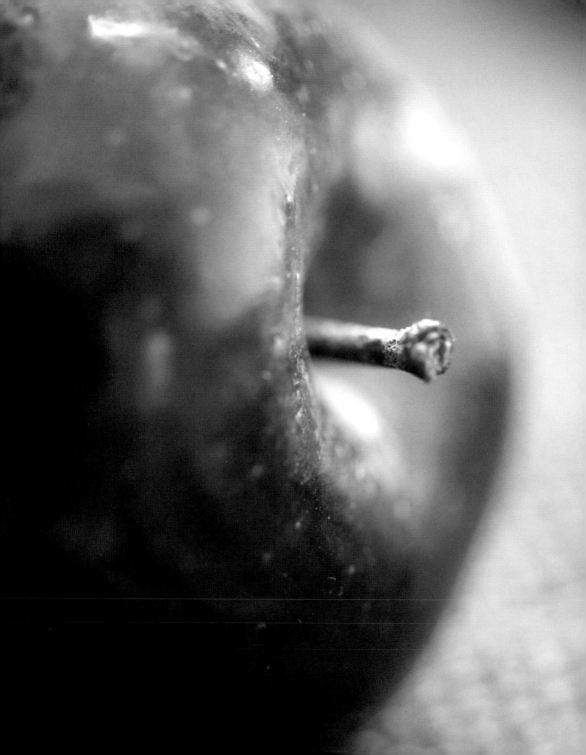

DRINKS MADE FROM APPLES AND PEARS

CIDER

To make cider, apples are pressed and the juice extracted from them is fermented. Most ciders are made from special cider apples, which are small, hard, and inedible, but eating and cooking apples can also be used—the mixture of fruit is an important factor in how a cider tastes. Once fermented, ciders are usually matured for several months to develop their full flavor. Although hard cider is also made outside England—in Spain's Basque region, where it's called *sidra*, and in Northern France—cider is a traditional

Apples are tumbled through water to wash them thoroughly before pressing (left). Traditional cider presses were big wooden contraptions and had to be capable of producing sufficient force to crush the fruit to a pulp (above). The fruit was pressed by hand several times to make sure all of the juice had been extracted. Modern plants use hydraulically operated plate presses.

CALVADOS

Calvados is a 40 percent ABV fruit brandy made from fermented apple juice (cider) in Normandy and Brittany in northern France. The making of calvados is governed by *appellation contrôlée* rules and it must be aged for at least two years. Although commonly served both before and after eating, in France, during a long meal, a small glass of calvados ("calva") is often drunk between courses to reinvigorate the appetite.

English drink. Production is centered in Somerset, Kent, Herefordshire, and Worcestershire.

Cider can be dry or sweet, still or sparkling, dark and cloudy or light and clear. Hard cider can have an ABV of anything from 2 to about 8 percent. It is made by large commercial producers and smaller concerns, and is available on draft and in bottles. Rough, local cider is called scrumpy.

Mass-produced hard ciders include the Irish brand, Magners, the first to introduce the concept of serving cider over ice, Merrydown, and Strongbow. In the United States, cider is nonalcoholic unless specifically termed "hard cider."

While the French have cornered the market in calvados, cider brandy or applejack, which is basically the same thing, has been produced in England since the seventeenth century and the finest vintages are said to rival the French variety in color, quality, and flavor.

APPLEJACK

Applejack is an American fruit brandy made from fermented apple juice (cider), with an ABV of around 40 percent.

PERRY

This traditional English drink is similar to cider except that it is made from fermented pear, rather than apple juice. The pears used are usually small, hard perry pears, rather than the dessert fruit, but not much perry is made, although Babycham (see below) is a popular commercial brand of sparkling perry.

BABYCHAM

Babycham is considered to be a rather "feminine" drink. It is a light sparkling perry with an ABV of 5.5 percent. It goes in and out of fashion in Britain, but is enduringly associated with the 1970's advertising slogan "I'll have a Babycham" and its jumping baby deer logo.

POIRE WILLIAM

Poire William is a French pear liqueur made by steeping Bartlett pears in pear brandy.

PERA SEGNANA

Pera Segnana is a similar Italian liqueur to Poire William.

These brandy stills, named Josephine and Fifi, were manufactured between the wars in Paris and are still used today to make cider brandy in England at Passvale Farm for the Somerset Cider Company.

DRINKS DERIVED FROM STARCH

Where to begin with beer? There are thousands of different beers and many different ways of making or brewing beer. Essentially, beer is fermented water and starch, although the exact constituents, including the minerals present in the water, all affect the style, appearance, and taste of the end product.

Beer can be made from wheat, rye, rice, potatoes, grasses such as sorghum, and many other raw ingredients, but the most common source of starch is malted barley. Malting involves encouraging the grains to germinate. After they begin to sprout they are dried. Malting helps develop the enzymes that generate the chemical reactions that are needed to turn the starch into sugar, which can then be fermented.

Beer may be flavored with a wide range of herbs and fruit, but the most common flavoring is hops, the flower of the hop vine. Hops impart a certain bitterness and also act as a preservative.

To cause fermentation, yeast is added, because this turns the sugar into alcohol and carbon dioxide. One particular type of yeast, known as brewer's yeast, has been used for centuries to make beer, but other types are also employed. Incidentally, brewer's yeast is a rich source of nutrients such as vitamin B, potassium, and selenium, so although their effectiveness is reduced by the brewing process, there is some foundation to the claim that beer has health-giving properties.

Various types of clarifying agents, such as isinglass, a substance obtained from the swim bladders of fish, or carrageenan, derived from seaweed, can be added to get remove the solid proteins from beer. In most beers, although not cask-conditioned ale and wheat beer, yeast sediment is also filtered out.

It is impossible to say who first brewed beer—it was probably invented by chance by various different societies at various different times—but 6,000 years ago the ancient Sumerians made it, and the Babylonians and Egyptians drank it too.

In medieval Europe monks did most of the brewing, because drinking was permitted during

In the last 30 years or so there has been a revolution among discerning beer drinkers in Britain and the United States, many of whom have rejected global brands in favor of local brews that have a more distinctive character. This has resulted in a thriving climate for smaller, regional brewers and "microbreweries" that produce beers suited to local tastes.

a fast and beer was nutritious. Indeed, monks in what is now Belgium are believed to have been the first people to flavor beer with hops.

In modern times, the industrial revolution and scientific progress, such as the discovery of pasteurization and refrigeration, meant that beer could be brewed more efficiently, with greater control over the process and on a larger scale.

The temperature at which beer is best enjoyed depends on the type of beer and personal preference. British beers such as bitter, stout, and pale ale are usually served at cellar temperature, and dark lager and wheat beer are usually lightly chilled, while lager tends to be chillled.

ALE

Ale is beer brewed from barley malt and flavored with hops. Types include bitter, brown ale, dark ale, and pale ale. The descriptors loosely relate to the color of the malt used, which is determined by how much and with what it is roasted. Ale is sometimes used as a general term to cover both beer and lager.

PALE ALE

Pale ale emerged in England in the early nineteenth century, when new technologies enabled brewers to use lighter colored malt to produce pale gold colored beer, known as pale ale. IPA (Indian Pale Ale), produced for export to the colonies, was both slightly more alcoholic, at least 4 percent ABV, and contained more hops, which helped keep the beer in good condition on long sea journeys. The popularity of bitter has since superseded that of pale ale in Britain, although IPA still survives.

century, but which is now hard to find. It is not drunk in the United States except in British-style pubs.

PORTER

Porter is a dark, bitter beer made from roasted, unmalted barley, which was very popular in the eighteenth century. Named for London's market workers, porter was generally strong, around 6 percent ABV, but the porter revival of recent years, led by small British brewers and microbreweries in the United States, has produced slightly less alcoholic porters with ABVs more likely to be around 4 percent.

STOUT

Stout is a type of porter and Guinness is indisputably the most famous brand of stout. Guinness was first brewed in Dublin in the mid-eighteenth century by Arthur Guinness. The way the barley is roasted gives Guinness its distinctive color and flavor. It has relatively low levels of carbon dioxide, so it is not particularly effervescent, but it contains nitrogen and it is the nitrogen bubbles that give it the characteristic creamy head. Guiness is popular around the globe but, of course, especially in Ireland. There are rumors that the version brewed in Ireland tastes different to that brewed in England.

DRAFT GUINNESS

Draft Guinness should be served chilled, but because of the way it foams, the glass should first be filled three-quarters of the way to the rim. Once it has settled, it can be filled up. Bartenders with a whimsical bent sometimes draw a picture in the head, perhaps a shamrock. Guinness is also sold in cans containing a widget that unleashes a stream of bubbles into the beer when the can is opened.

BITTER

Bitter is a style of beer that arose in Britain in the late nineteenth century, as brewers started to develop beers that could be made and sold quickly. It grew out of pale ale, but had a deeper bronze color due to the use of slightly darker malt.

Theoretically, bitter has an ABV of between 3.4 and 3.9 percent, while best bitter is stronger and has an ABV of 4 percent upward. However, the names of commercial products can sometimes be misleading. "Extra" or "special strong" bitter should have an ABV of 5 percent upward. The terms "beer" and "bitter" are often used interchangeably in England.

MILD

Mild is a style of beer that was once very popular in Britain, starting in the first half of the twentieth

Murphy's is another brand of dry stout, while Mackeson is an example of a sweet stout.

CASK-CONDITIONED ALE

Cask-conditioned ale is unfiltered and unpasteurized beer. The yeast is left in the barrel, so fermentation continues, giving the beer a fresh, just-brewed taste.

BARLEY WINE

Barley wine is actually a beer, that is dark and fruity, with a high alcohol content.

LAGER

One of the main differences between beer and lager is that beer is brewed at higher temperatures with top-fermenting yeast (the yeast rises to the top of the vessel in which the beer is being brewed), while lager is brewed at lower temperatures with bottom-fermenting yeast. In fact, the name comes from the German word *lagern*, meaning "to store," because lager is stored for at least a few weeks, certainly longer than most other beers, in order to complete the fermentation process.

The malt used in lager tends to be lighter, so, compared to beer, lager has a lighter color and a crisper, less hoppy flavor. Lager also tends to be more effervescent and has a lower alcohol content, although of course there are plenty of strong lagers available. It is generally served chilled.

Lager was first brewed in Germany, in Bavaria, in the sixteenth century. The style developed because brewers stopped making beer in the summer, when the heat made it unstable and likely to go bad. Instead, they stored their winter brews in caves and cellars, often chilling them with blocks of ice. They discovered that, in these colder temperatures, the yeast sunk to the bottom and the beer—now lager—was more stable.

The Germans take their lager seriously and in 1516 introduced the world's first food law—the *Reinheitsgebot* or Purity Law. This governs the ingredients of beer and states that beer may only be produced from barley, hops, and water. Of course, the addition of yeast is now permitted, but otherwise the law remains the same and German brewers are obliged to obey it. This is why German beers and lagers are generally so clear and of such high quality. Malt liquor is an Amerian type of extra-strong lager with an artificially induced high alcohol content, too alcoholic to be marketed as beer.

PILSNER

Pilsner is a style of lager that was developed in Pilsen, in what is now the Czech Republic, in the mid-nineteenth century. The town's brewers hired a Bavarian lager expert called Josef Groll to improve their product. He let them into the secrets of German brewing, but the use of local ingredients, in particular the local soft water, and light barley, gave rise to a light, clear, relatively carbonated drink, that subsequently became known as pilsner. Most modern pale lagers are based on the pilsner style.

Bock

Broadly speaking, bock is a heavier, darker (contrasted with pale) style of German lager, originally brewed in the north German town of Einbeck, but now made in many variants across Germany, Austria, and the Netherlands.

Ice beer

Not to be confused with the recent trend for extra-cold beers, ice beer is not colder than normal lager, but it is slightly stronger. The brew is chilled so that the water in it starts to freeze, but not the alcohol. Ice crystals are then skimmed off, resulting in less dilution and therefore greater strength. This method is how some of the world's strongest beers are made,

In the past ten years the global consumption of beer, in particular bottled lager, has increased dramatically. In 2004, more than 33 million gallons were consumed worldwide with drinkers in China, the United States, and Germany leading the way. The biggest beer producer in the world is Anheuser-Busch, which produces Budweiser among many brands, but the most widely available beer is the Dutch Heineken.

such as the traditional German *Eisboch* EKU, which has an ABV as high as 13.5 percent.

Steam beer

This gets its name from the high level of carbonation in the beer which causes a hissing noise when casks are opened. The effervescence is due to use of the lager method, with yeast at the bottom, combined with the higher temperatures used in ale brewing.

BEER AND LAGER BRANDS

❖ **Adnams** is a Suffolk-based brewer, which produces a bitter, the higher ABV Explorer, and a range of seasonal beers, including Old Ale and Oyster Stout.
❖ **Asahi** is a Japanese brand of lager, well-known for

Asahi Super Dry, which was one of the first of the lighter lagers to be produced in Japan.
❖ **Beck's** is a German brand of lager. Its Bremen-based parent company is a major exporter and makes dark beers and citrus-flavored drinks too.
❖ **Belhaven** is a brewer based just outside Edinburgh, Scotland, which produces a range of beers, including St. Andrews Ale and Belhaven 80 Shilling (the strength of Scottish beers used to be measured as 70, 80, or 90 shillings).
❖ **Boddingtons** bitter was originally brewed at the Strangeways Brewery in Manchester, England, but is now made in several locations and sold worldwide.
❖ **Brahma** is a Brazilian brand of lager.
❖ **Brains** is a Cardiff-based brewer, which produces a range of beers, including Bread of Heaven and seasonal beers such as Land of My Fathers and St. David's Ale.
❖ **Budweiser** is an American brand of lager, owned by the Anheuser-Busch company. Bud, as it is colloquially known, and Bud Light, which has a lower ABV and calorie count, are among the top-selling lagers in the world.
❖ **Budweiser Budvar** is a Czech lager, also brewed in Britain, but not to be confused with the well-

known North American lager Budweiser—the right to the name Budweiser has been the subject of legal action in several countries.

❖ **Carling** is a lager, formerly known as Carling Black Label and famous for the slogan "I bet he drinks Carling Black Label."

❖ **Carlsberg's** parent company is headquartered in Copenhagen, Denmark, although the lager is brewed at various sites around the world. The same company also makes Special Brew, a strong canned lager with an ABV of 9 percent.

❖ **Cobra** is an Indian lager, also brewed in Britain.

❖ **Coors** is a North American brand of lager, with many sub-brands.

❖ **Corona** is a Mexican brand of lager, often served with a wedge of lemon or lime inserted into the neck of the bottle, although this isn't the custom in Mexico.

❖ **Dos Equis** is a brand of Mexican lager.

❖ **Efes** is a Turkish brand of pilsner-style lager.

❖ **Fosters** is an Australian brand of lager, although brewed locally in Britain and other countries, where it is more popular than in its native Australia.

❖ **Freedom** is a British brand of organic microbrewed lager and pilsner.

❖ **Fuller's** is a west London-based brewer, which produces a range of beers, including London Pride and seasonal beers such as Jack Frost and London Porter.

❖ **Greene King** is a Suffolk-based brewer, which produces Greene King IPA and owns sub-brands that include Abbot Ale, Old Speckled Hen, and Ruddles County.

❖ **Grolsch** is a Dutch brand of lager, which is bottled with a distinctive, old-fashioned-looking swing-top cap and has a range of sub-brands.

❖ **Heineken** is a Dutch brand of lager, brewed at various sites around the world and with a range of sub-brands.

❖ **Kaliber** is a British alcohol-free lager that's made as a full-strength lager, but at the end of the brewing process all the alcohol is removed.

❖ **Kingfisher** is an Indian brand of lager.

❖ **Kronenbourg 1664** is a French brand of lager.

❖ **Marstons** is a brewer based in Burton-upon-Trent, England, that produces a range of beers, including Burton Bitter and Pedigree.

❖ **McEwans** is an Edinburgh-based brand of beer and lager, part of Scottish Newcastle plc.

❖ **Michelob** is an American brand of lager with a range of sub-brands.

❖ **Miller** is a brand of American lager. Its parent company has a range of sub-brands, including the low-alcohol Miller Lite.

❖ **Moretti** is an Italian lager, similar in style to German bock.

❖ **Newcastle Brown Ale** is a brand of dark, mild bottled beer.

❖ **Peroni** is an Italian brand of lager, the most famous product being Nastro Azzurro.

❖ **Pilsner Urquell** is a brand of Czech lager.

❖ **Red Stripe** is a Jamaican brand of lager, brewed locally in Britain.

❖ **Rolling Rock** is an American brand of lager. Some believe the 33 on the label relates to the repeal of prohibition in the United States in 1933, but it's more likely to be a reference to the drink's original slogan, which was thirty-three words long. A printer allegedly incorporated the number into the slogan by mistake.

❖ **Sagres** is a Portuguese brand of lager, brewed in the south of the country.

❖ **Sam Smith** is a Yorkshire-based brewer, producing a range of beers, including Old Brewery Bitter.

❖ **Sapporo** is a Japanese brand of lager brewed since 1877, initially by a brewmaster who had studied the art of beer making in Germany. It is now brewed all over the world.

❖ **San Miguel** is a brand of Spanish lager.

❖ **Sol** is a brand of Mexican lager.

❖ **Staropramen** is a strong Czech lager.

❖ **Steinlager** is a New Zealand lager.

❖ **Stella Artois** is a Belgian lager, brewed at various sites around the world.

- ❖ **Super Bock** is a Portuguese brand of lager, brewed in the north of the country.
- ❖ **Tennent's** is a strong Scottish lager, with a high 9 percent ABV.
- ❖ **Tetley** makes a range of Yorkshire beers, not to be confused with the tea of the same name.
- ❖ **Theakston** is a North Yorkshire-based brewer, which produces a range of beers, including the fairly strong Old Peculier and seasonal beers such as Hogshead Bitter.
- ❖ **Tiger** is a brand of lager, originally from Hong Kong, now brewed at various sites in southeast Asia.
- ❖ **Wychwood** is an Oxfordshire-based brewer that produces a range of beers, including Legendary Hobgoblin and seasonal beers such as BeeWyched, brewed with Fairtrade honey.
- ❖ **Young's** is a south London-based brewer that produces a range of beers, including Young's Bitter, Waggledance, and Wells Bombardier.
- ❖ **Zima** is an alcopop or, according to its producer, a malt beverage that's similar to lager. It is available in three citrus flavors.

BELGIAN BEER

Belgium has a rich and varied brewing tradition. For example, it makes well-respected and somewhat unusual wheat beer, red beer, brown ale, Trappist, and lambic beer, the latter being particularly prized by connoisseurs. How Belgian beer is served and drunk is heavily ritualized, and many brewers produce their own branded glasses, in shapes supposedly suitable for their type of brew. Belgian beer tends to be considerably stronger than the beer commonly drunk in the United Kingdom and the United States. It is not unusual to find ABVs of 10 and 11 percent.

Unsurprisingly, wheat beer contains a lot of wheat, although many wheat beers also contain malted barley. The style is generally associated with Belgium, where it's called *withieren,* and Germany, where it's called *weissbier.* Both names actually mean "white beer." This is a reference to their light color, which comes from the yeast sediment. Wheat beers are sometimes a little sweet and sometimes a little fruity. They are also fairly light on the palate and have an ABV of around 5 percent. Hoegaarden is a well-known brand.

To qualify as Trappist, a beer must be brewed by Trappist monks, or at least made under their direct supervision. There are six Trappist breweries in Belgium. These are Achel, Chimay, Orval, Rochefort, Westmalle, Westvleteren, and La Trappe. (There is also a Trappist brewery in the Netherlands, called La Trappe.) The monks originally made beer for their own consumption, as a source of nourishment, especially during fasts and because the water wasn't safe to drink, but now beer production of beer gives the abbeys a substantial income.

Lambic is only brewed in Belgium, in an area called Paylottenland southwest of Brussels. Rather than being fermented with brewer's yeast, lambic is a style of beer that's produced by a process called spontaneous fermentation, in which the beer is exposed to airborne wild yeasts. This gives it a sour, almost ciderlike flavor.

DRINKS DISTILLED FROM SUGAR

RUM

Today, rum is made all over the world, but it is most strongly associated with the Caribbean, where it was first made in the seventeenth century by the slaves who worked on the sugarcane plantations.

Rum is made by fermenting and then distilling molasses, the thick, syrupy by-product of sugarcane processing. The resulting liquid is clear and is usually described as light, white, or silver rum, but this is

often aged in oak barrels or colored with caramel to make dark, amber, golden, or black rum.

There is no a single standard for rum production, individual countries have their own, and similar styles of rum can have different names, even within the Caribbean. For this reason it's hard to give a firm ABV for rum, but it's generally around 40 percent, although if a rum is described as overproof it could have an ABV of approaching double that percentage.

Rum can be made into a liqueur or cordial and spiced or flavored with citrus fruit, mango, or coconut. It is the basis for a number of well-known cocktails, for instance the Cuba Libre, Mai Tai, Daiquiri and, of course, Rum Punch. Rum is often used as the basis for a mixed drink, with, say, cola, and it can also be drunk straight, with or without ice.

RUM BRANDS

❖ **Appleton Estate** is a brand of aged Jamaican rum.
❖ **Bacardi** is a brand of white rum. The Bacardi company was originally founded in Cuba in the late ninteenth century, but the family that owns it left after the Cuban Revolution of 1959 and the business is now based in Bermuda. It has offshoots all over the Caribbean and throughout the world. As well as various rums, Bacardi makes the Bacardi Breezer range of alcopop premixed rum and fruit drinks that are popular with young people.

❖ **Malibu** is not a pure rum. It is a white, rum-based liqueur with a strong coconut flavor, although versions with additional fruit flavorings are also available. Made in Barbados, it has an ABV of 21 percent and can be served straight, with ice, or mixed with soda pop. Its distinctive logo, on a white-painted bottle, consists of crossed palm trees against a setting sun.

❖ **Mount Gay** is a brand of Barbadian rum, first produced in 1703 and available in several styles and flavors.

❖ **Wray and Nephews** is a brand of Jamaican rum. Wray and Nephews White Overproof rum has a rather high ABV of 63 percent.

❖ **Wood's Old Navy** is a brand of Guyanan rum. Its makers claim it has the highest ABV—57 percent—of any rum on the market.

CACHAÇA

This sugarcane spirit or rum is the national drink of Brazil, being the most popular distilled alcoholic beverage in that country, and it is an essential ingredient in the classic cocktail, the Caipirinha. White cachaça is unaged, while dark cachaça, seen as the premium version, is aged in wooden barrels.

CHOCOLATE LIQUEUR BRANDS

❖ **Ashanti Gold** is a Danish chocolate liqueur.

❖ **Creme de cacao** is a syrupy chocolate liqueur flavored with cocoa and vanilla beans that has an ABV of between 25 and 30 percent. It is usually clear, but dark crème de cacao is caramel-colored.

❖ **Godiva** is a chocolate liqueur with a 17 percent ABV, which comes in dark, milk, white, and mocha.

❖ **Mozart** is a milk chocolate liqueur from Austria, also available in dark and white chocolate versions.

❖ **Sabra** is a chocolate-and-orange-flavored liqueur, from Israel.

❖ **Barbancourt** is a brand of Haitian rum or rhum, as it says on the label, that is made from sugarcane juice, rather than molasses, and, like cognac, it is double-distilled.

❖ **Captain Morgan** is a brand of dark rum, named for a Welsh-born pirate who sailed the Spanish Main called Sir Henry Morgan.

❖ **Havana Club** is a brand of Cuban rum. Founded in the late nineteenth century, Havana Club was nationalized after the Cuban Revolution of 1959. Its various rums, including some prized aged varieties, are sold around the world by the Cuban government, in a joint venture with the makers of Pernod and Ricard.

❖ **Gomme syrup** is a nonalcoholic syrup made of sugar and water, and thickened with gum arabic, used to sweeten cocktails.

❖ **Orgeat syrup** is a nonalcoholic, almond-flavored syrup used to sweeten cocktails.

❖ **Sour mix** is a mixture of sugar syrup and lemon juice, also known as sweet and sour mix or bar mix.

❖ **Sugar syrup** is used for sweetening drinks. This is liquid sugar and it can be either clear or brown. It can be bought commercially or homemade by dissolving two parts sugar in one part water (see recipe on page 15). Sugar syrup can also be called simple syrup, simple sugar syrup or bar syrup.

To get the alcohol into a liqueur chocolate, boiling sugar syrup is poured onto the alcohol. The mixture is cooled for more than 15 hours. As it cools, the sugar crystalizes into a shell around the alcohol. After they are completely cooled, the capsules are carefully removed from the molds, brushed with melted dark chocolate, then thickly coated with it. The manufacturing process takes at least two days.

NONALCOHOLIC FLAVORINGS MADE WITH SUGAR

❖ **Cordial** is a sweet, fruit-flavored syrup, generally nonalcoholic, that is diluted to taste or used in a cocktail. In the United States, cordial is sometimes used to mean a liqueur.

DRINKS DISTILLED FROM AGAVE

MEZCAL

This is a distilled spirit made from a succulent (not a cactus, by the way) called agave. Mezcal is produced throughout Mexico, but particularly around Oaxaca. Foreign bodies are often added to bottles of mezcal (mescal), the most famous being a "worm." It isn't really a worm, it is either a weevil or the larva of a moth.

TEQUILA

A mezcal produced exclusively in the Jalisco region of Mexico, tequila is made from the roasted heart of the blue agave, one of the 136 species of the agave plant that grow in Mexico. This plant takes around a decade to mature and produce its pure white flowers.

The forerunner of tequila was called pulque, a beerlike fermented agave drink made by the indigenous Mexicans, but when the Spanish Conquistadors arrived in the sixteenth century they soon developed a stronger tipple by distilling agave syrup. Tequila is usually distilled twice, which gives it an ABV of around 40 percent.

Tequila is drunk straight, often from a special narrow glass called a *caballito*. In Mexico it is not downed in one with a lick of salt and a suck of lime as for a Tequila Slammer.

Tequila has five classifications. The original, and most common, is *blanco* (white) or *plata* (silver), in which the spirit is not aged and consequently can be harsh and raw, although it may have more agave flavor than other types. The second type is *oro* (gold) tequila, which is essentially *blanco* with coloring and flavoring added, to make it look older and taste smoother. Next is *reposado* (rested), which is aged for up to a year in wooden casks. This darkens the color and the tequila takes on flavoring from the wood. *Anejo* (vintage) is aged from one to ten years, generally making it even darker and more woody. Finally, there is *extra anejo* (ultra-aged), that is kept in cask for a minimum of three years and, again, up to ten.

There are also two other categories of tequila—100 percent agave or *puro de agave*, which is what the connoisseurs usually prefer, and simple tequila, which is also known as *mixto*. This contains just over 50 percent agave, the rest being other fermented sugars. If the label doesn't say 100 percent agave, then it isn't. Well-known brands of tequila include José Cuervo and Sauza.

SOTOL

Sotol is a distilled spirit similar to mezcal, made in the Chihuahua area of Mexico from a plant called the desert spoon (*Dasylirion wheeleri*). It is rarely exported.

DRINKS DISTILLED FROM RICE

SAKE

Although it is commonly described as Japanese rice wine, saké is much more like rice beer, due to the way in which it is fermented, which is much closer to

the process used for beer. The first saké was probably made by people chewing and then spitting out rice, so that their saliva activated natural fermentation. However, at some point in history a mold was discovered that enabled the mastication stage to be bypassed and today sake production is appropriately high-tech.

Sake is generally filtered, so it is clear, but needless to say there are many different types of sake, some not even made from rice. It tends to be served straight. Sake is unusual in that it is an alcoholic drink that can be consumed cold, warm, or hot, depending on the season, the quality of the sake, and the drinker's own preference. It is traditionally poured from a flask into a shallow cup, and there are many Japanese rituals associated with it. For instance, drinking from someone else's cup apparently signals friendship.

SHOCHU

Shochu is a clear Japanese spirit distilled from rice or sweet potato wine. It is similar to vodka.

SOJU

Soju is a clear spirit from Korea, distilled from fermented rice, but similar in taste to a slightly sweet vodka, with an ABV of between 20 and 45 percent.

DRINKS MADE FROM BEANS AND LEAVES

COFFEE

To make coffee, the roasted and ground beans of the coffee plant are steeped in hot water. There are a range of methods for doing this, including filtering, percolating, or using an espresso machine, and a whole culture and set of rituals surround this process. Coffee is often used to flavor liqueurs. Hot coffee mixed with Irish whiskey and sugar, and topped with whipped cream, makes the after-dinner drink Irish coffee.

Well-known coffee liqueurs include Kahlúa, a Mexican 25 percent ABV, and Tia Maria, a rum-based Jamaican 26.5 percent ABV coffee liqueur flavored with the finest Jamaican Blue Mountain coffee beans.

Coffee contains caffeine, as do most colas and Red Bull, a proprietory brand of nonalcoholic, sparkling, energy drink. Along with the caffeine, Red Bull also contains an amino acid derivative called taurine. It's drunk to combat physical and mental exhaustion, but is also commonly mixed with spirits.

TEA

Tea is made from the dried leaves of the tea bush, a member of the camellia family, infused in hot water. Sugar, and sometimes milk or lemon, are generally added to the hot beverage, but it can also be chilled and drunk black, sweetened with sugar, and served with a slice of lemon. This is known as iced tea. Cold, weak tea is sometimes used as an ingredient in a Long Island Iced Tea cocktail.

TYPES OF WATER

MINERAL WATER

Essentially mineral water is water containing minerals, such as salts. Those minerals may be present in natural spring water or they can be added when the water is bottled, although most countries have regulations governing the production of mineral water. Likewise, mineral water can be still—without effervescence—or it may be naturally carbonated or carbon dioxide can be added. Carbonated mineral water is also known as sparkling water. Club soda is very similar, but is more likely to have added salts, particularly sodium bicarbonate. Club soda is also known as seltzer water.

American brands of mineral water include Poland Spring, Saratoga Springs, and Calistoga. French brands include Evian and Volvic, which are both still, and Perrier, which is sparkling. San Pellegrino is an Italian brand of sparkling mineral water.

TONIC WATER

This carbonated water contains quinine, originally added to protect against malaria, rife in the drink's initial target markets of Africa and India (the product is sometimes known as Indian tonic water). However, modern versions contain only tiny amounts of quinine. This gives the drink a bitter-sweet taste, but enables it to mix well with gin and vodka. Canada Dry and Schweppes are well-known brands of tonic water.

WAKE-UP CALL

Although not to be recommended, a cocktail can be just the way to start the day, particularly during the weekend when you've a lazy day ahead of you. Fruity, fizzy, creamy, or caffeine-based, any of the recipes featured here will make a perfect accompaniment to that late breakfast or leisurely brunch.

BANANA DAIQUIRI ◄ ☆ ▢ 🍸

Rum and lime juice are the basis for a classic Daiquiri. Here, the addition of bananas and cream make for a rich and fortifying version.

SERVES 1
2 measures white rum
½ measure triple sec
½ measure lime juice
½ measure light cream
1 teaspoon sugar syrup
¼ banana, peeled and sliced
wedge of lime

In a blender, process the white rum, triple sec, lime juice, cream, sugar syrup, and banana until smooth. Then pour the mixture, without straining, into a chilled cocktail glass or lowball glass and dress with the wedge of lime.

Famously a favorite of American writer Ernest Hemingway and President John F. Kennedy, the Daiquiri is named for a small town in Cuba. It was allegedly invented at the turn of the twentieth century by an American engineer, who was working there, but ran out of gin and resorted to rum. Given the prevalence of rum in Cuba, however, it is probable that the locals had discovered this delicious drink quite some time earlier.

Rum, lime juice, and a little sugar or syrup are the basis for a classic Daiquiri, but you can blend the drink with ice to make a frozen Daiquiri or add just about any kind of fruit.

Whatever else goes into a Daiquiri, though, it is important to squeeze the lime by hand so that the oils from the peel mix with the juice and impart a sharp, intense flavor to the cocktail.

MAIDEN'S PRAYER ▾

This is similar to a Chelsea Sidecar (page 168), but the orange juice in a Maiden's Prayer will give you an extra little sugar rush too.

SERVES 1
1 measure gin
1 measure triple sec
1 teaspoon orange juice
1 teaspoon lemon juice
twist of lemon peel

Shake the gin, triple sec, orange juice, and lemon juice vigorously over ice cubes until well frosted, and strain into a chilled cocktail glass. Garnish with the twist of lemon peel.

It's not clear quite why the bride's mother should favor this tipple. The combination of sloe gin and London gin gives it a delicious flavor and some potency.

BRIDE'S MOTHER ▸

SERVES 1
1½ measures sloe gin
1 measure London gin
2½ measures grapefruit juice
½ measure sugar syrup
lemon slice

Shake the sloe gin, gin, grapefruit juice, and sugar syrup vigorously over ice cubes until well frosted, and strain into a chilled cocktail glass with the slice of lemon.

SEVENTH HEAVEN ◀

SERVES 1

2 measures gin

½ measure maraschino

½ measure grapefruit juice

fresh mint sprig

Shake the gin, maraschino, and grapefruit juice
vigorously over ice cubes until well frosted. Strain into
a chilled cocktail glass and dress with the fresh mint.

MELON BALL ◀

SERVES 1

2 measures vodka

2 measures Midori

4 measures pineapple juice

cracked ice

melon wedge

Pour the vodka, Midori, and pineapple juice over ice
cubes and stir well to mix. Half-fill a chilled highball glass
with cracked ice and strain the cocktail over it. Decorate
with the wedge of melon.

MELON STATE BALL ▾

SERVES 1
2 measures vodka
1 measure Midori
2 measures orange juice

Pour the vodka, Midori, and orange juice over ice cubes and shake vigorously until well frosted. Strain into a chilled cocktail glass.

GENOA VODKA ▴

SERVES 1
2 measures vodka
1 measure Campari
3 measures orange juice
orange slice

Shake the vodka, Campari ,and orange juice vigorously over ice cubes until well frosted. Strain into a small chilled lowball glass and dress with the slice of orange.

LAST MANGO IN PARIS ◀

SERVES 1
2 measures vodka
1 measure framboise (raspberry liqueur)
1 measure lime juice
½ mango, peeled, pitted, and chopped
2 strawberries, halved
lime slice
1 whole strawberry

Mix the vodka, framboise, lime juice, mango and halved strawberries in a blender until slushy. Pour into a chilled cocktail glass or sour glass and dress with the slice of lime and the extra strawberry.

BLUE MONDAY

The lovely color and fruity flavor of this cocktail is guaranteed to make Monday your favorite day of the week.

SERVES 1
cracked ice
1 measure vodka
½ measure Cointreau
1 tablespoon blue curaçao

Put the cracked ice into a mixing glass or pitcher, and add the vodka, Cointreau, and curaçao. Stir well and strain into a cocktail glass.

LADY

SERVES 1
2 measures gin
1 measure peach brandy
1 measure lemon juice
1 teaspoon egg white

Shake the gin, peach brandy, and lemon juice over ice cubes with the egg white until well frosted. Strain into a chilled cocktail glass.

BEAGLE ▾

SERVES 1
cracked ice
dash of kümmel
dash of lemon juice
2 measures brandy
1 measure cranberry juice

Put the cracked ice into a mixing glass. Add the dash of kümmel and the dash of lemon juice, then pour in the brandy and cranberry juice. Stir well to mix and strain into a chilled cocktail glass.

WALK TALL

This looks and smells like orange juice, but don't be deceived, there is plenty of alcohol.

SERVES 1
½ measure sweet white vermouth
¼ measure gin
¼ measure Campari
¼ measure orange liqueur
sweet orange juice
club soda (optional)
orange peel

Mix the vermouth, gin, Campari, orange liqueur, and orange juice well, and pour into a highball glass full of ice cubes. Top with a splash of club soda if you like and decorate with a twist of orange peel.

BACHELOR'S BAIT ▸

SERVES 1
2 measures gin
1 teaspoon grenadine
1 egg white
dash of orange bitters

Shake the gin, grenadine, and egg white together over ice cubes until well frosted. Add a dash of orange bitters, give the mixture another quick shake, and strain into a chilled cocktail glass.

STRAWBERRY COLADA ◀

SERVES 1
4–6 ice cubes, crushed
3 measures golden rum
4 measures pineapple juice
1 measure coconut cream
6 strawberries, hulled
pineapple wedge
extra strawberries

In a blender, mix together the crushed ice, rum, pineapple juice, coconut cream, and hulled strawberries. Blend until smooth, then, without straining, pour into a chilled highball glass. Dress with the wedge of pineapple and a few strawberries.

This version of a Piña Colada, which literally means "strained pineapple," is made extra fruity—and somewhat pinkish—by the delicious addition of strawberries.

ESPRESSO GALLIANO ▲

This variant on an Irish Coffee is an excellent way to start the day, but it tastes best without the traditional cream.

SERVES 1
2 measures Galliano
freshly made strong black coffee
sugar to taste
lemon or orange juice
sugar
twist of orange peel

Put the Galliano into a warmed, heatproof glass. Add the coffee, a teaspoon or two of sugar, and a splash of lemon or orange juice to taste, and stir. Serve with the twist of orange peel.

WEDDING BELLE ▶

Whether bride, groom, or one of the guests, this will make you ready for the big day.

SERVES 1

2 measures gin

2 measures Dubonnet

1 measure cherry brandy

1 measure orange juice

twist of orange peel

Shake the gin, Dubonnet, cherry brandy, and orange juice over ice cubes until well frosted. Strain into a cocktail glass and serve with the twist of orange peel.

BLOODY MARY

SERVES 1

cracked ice

2 measures vodka

4 measures tomato juice

½ measure lemon juice

2 dashes of Worcestershire sauce

dash of Tabasco sauce

celery salt

black pepper

lemon wedge

celery stalk

Shake the vodka, tomato juice, lemon juice, Worcestershire sauce, and Tabasco vigorously over cracked ice. Season with the celery salt and black pepper. Strain into an iced old-fashioned glass and dress with the wedge of lemon and stalk of celery.

IS THIS ALL? ▶

Suffice to say that this citrus combination is more than enough to fill your morning with optimism.

SERVES 1

2 measures lemon vodka

1 measure triple sec

1 measure lemon juice

1 egg white

Shake the lemon vodka, triple sec, lemon juice, and egg white over ice cubes until well frosted. Strain into a chilled cocktail glass.

FUZZY MARTINI ▲

SERVES 1
2 measures vanilla vodka
½ measure coffee vodka
1 teaspoon peach schnapps
peach slice

Shake the vanilla vodka, coffee vodka, and peach schnapps over ice cubes until well frosted. Strain into a chilled cocktail glass and dress with the slice of peach.

GOLDEN FLIP ▲

Sherry and almond liqueur are the bases for this flip, with an added kick of vodka.

SERVES 1
1 measure vodka
1 measure sweet sherry
1 measure amaretto
1 egg yolk
1 tablespoon superfine sugar
grated nutmeg

Shake all of the ingredients except the nutmeg over ice cubes until frosted. Strain into a chilled wine glass and sprinkle with freshly grated nutmeg.

THIS IS IT

Is it? See what you think.

SERVES 1
cracked ice
2 measures gin
1 measure triple sec
1 measure lemon juice
1 egg white

Shake the gin, triple sec, lemon juice, and egg white vigorously over cracked ice until well frosted, then strain the mixture into a chilled cocktail glass.

POLYNESIA

SERVES 1
cracked ice
2 measures white rum
2 measures passion fruit juice
1 measure lime juice
1 egg white
dash of Angostura bitters

Shake the rum, passion fruit juice, lime juice, and egg white over cracked ice, with a dash of Angostura bitters, until well frosted. Strain into a chilled cocktail glass.

APPLE BLOSSOM ◄

SERVES 1
2 measures brandy
1½ measures apple juice
½ teaspoon lemon juice
lemon slice

Pour the brandy, apple juice, and lemon juice over ice cubes in a mixing glass and stir well. Half-fill a chilled lowball glass with ice cubes and strain the cocktail over them. Dress with the slice of lemon.

PASSIONATE DAIQUIRI ◂ 🍸

This twist on the traditional Daiquiri introduces the delicate flavor of passion fruit to the rum and lime.

SERVES 1

2 measures white rum
1 measure lime juice
½ measure passion fruit syrup
1 cocktail cherry

Pour the rum, lime juice, and passion fruit syrup over ice cubes and shake vigorously until well frosted. Strain into a chilled cocktail glass and decorate with the cocktail cherry.

CREAMY SCREWDRIVER ▴ 🍹

By adding a protein-rich egg yolk, to the classic Screwdriver (page 296) you'll be all set for the day.

SERVES 1

2 measures vodka
crushed ice
6 measures orange juice
1 egg yolk
½ teaspoon sugar syrup
cracked ice
orange slice

In a blender mix the vodka, crushed ice, orange juice, egg yolk and sugar syrup until smooth. Half-fill a chilled highball glass with cracked ice and pour the cocktail over it without straining. Serve with the slice of orange.

TITANIC ▾

A genuine iceberg adds authenticity, but if you can't get it, ordinary cracked ice works perfectly well too.

SERVES 1
3 measures mandarin liqueur
2 measures vodka
cracked ice
sparkling water

Shake the mandarin liqueur and vodka vigorously over ice cubes until well frosted. Half-fill a chilled highball glass or lowball glass with cracked ice and strain the cocktail over it. Fill with sparkling water.

SLOW COMFORTABLE SCREW ☆

SERVES 1
2 measures sloe gin
orange juice
cracked ice
orange slice

Shake the sloe gin and orange juice with the cracked ice until well frosted and pour into a chilled highball glass. Decorate with the slice of orange.

The simple, classic "Screw" has given rise to numerous and increasingly elaborate variations. You should always use freshly squeezed orange juice, however, to make this refreshing cocktail—it's just not the same with packaged juice.

MEXICOLA

SERVES 1
cracked ice
2 measures tequila
1 measure lime juice
cola
lime or lemon slice

*Half-fill a chilled highball glass with the cracked ice.
Pour the tequila and lime juice over the ice and top
up with cola. Stir gently and decorate with the slice
of lime or lemon.*

BOURBON MILK PUNCH

SERVES 1
2 measures bourbon
3 measures milk
1 teaspoon clear honey
dash of vanilla extract
freshly grated nutmeg

*Shake the bourbon, milk, honey, and vanilla extract over
ice cubes until well frosted. Strain into a chilled highball
glass or lowball glass and sprinkle with the freshly
grated nutmeg.*

LEMON SHERBET ▸ 🔲 🔲

This turns into a delicious, fluffy, thick drink that you might need to eat with a spoon.

SERVES 1

2 measures gin
1 measure lemon juice
1 measure cream
½ measure orange curaçao
1 teaspoon superfine sugar
dash of orange flower water
a little crushed ice

Mix all the ingredients together in a blender for 10–15 seconds. Pour into a chilled lowball glass or highball glass and serve with straws.

DIAMOND FIZZ 🍸

SERVES 1

2 measures gin
½ measure lemon juice
1 teaspoon sugar syrup
champagne, chilled

Shake the gin, lemon juice, and sugar syrup over ice cubes until well frosted. Strain into a chilled champagne flute and fill with the chilled champagne.

KIRSCH RICKEY ▸ 🔲

The main characteristic of a Rickey is that it is refreshingly sharp, but here the kirsch and fresh cherries add just a tiny hint of sweetness.

SERVES 1

crushed ice
2 measures kirsch
1 tablespoon lime juice
sparkling water
a few fresh cherries or olives, pitted

Pour the kirsch and lime juice into a chilled lowball glass, half-filled with crushed ice. Fill with sparkling water and stir gently. Decorate with the pitted fresh cherries or olives.

MISSISSIPPI MULE ◄

The Mississippi Mule shares no ingredients with its better-known cousin the Moscow Mule (page 156), but it delivers quite a kick nonetheless.

SERVES 1

2 measures gin
½ measure crème de cassis
½ measure lemon juice

Shake the gin, crème de cassis, and lemon juice vigorously over ice cubes until well frosted, and strain into a small chilled lowball glass.

HARLEM ▲

SERVES 1

2 measures gin
1½ measures pineapple juice
1 teaspoon maraschino
1 tablespoon fresh pineapple, chopped
pineapple leaf

Shake the gin, pineapple juice, and maraschino over ice cubes. Add the chopped fresh pineapple and shake again until well frosted. Strain into a chilled lowball glass and garnish with the pineapple leaf.

ORANGE BLOSSOM

SERVES 1
cracked ice
2 measures gin
2 measures orange juice
orange slice

Shake the gin and orange juice vigorously over the cracked ice until well frosted. Strain into a chilled cocktail glass and decorate with the slice of orange.

CHANGUIRONGO ▲

SERVES 1
cracked ice
2 measures white tequila
ginger ale
lime or lemon slice

Half-fill a chilled highball glass with cracked ice. Add the tequila and fill with the ginger ale. Stir gently and dress with the slice of lime or lemon.

During Prohibition, the gin served in speakeasies was often literally made in the bathtub and flavored with fresh orange juice to conceal its filthy flavor. Made with good quality gin, which needs no such concealment, the Orange Blossom is delightfully refreshing.

DUKE ▲   🍷

A Buck's Fizz—simply orange juice and champagne—is a gently refreshing cocktail. The Duke is similar, but the addition of triple sec ups the orange flavor, the alcohol content—and the vigor of the alarm call.

SERVES 1
1 measure triple sec
½ measure lemon juice
½ measure orange juice
1 egg white
dash of maraschino
champagne or sparkling wine, chilled

Shake the triple sec, lemon juice, orange juice, egg white, and a dash of maraschino vigorously over ice cubes until well frosted. Strain into a chilled wine glass and fill with the chilled champagne or sparkling wine.

MILLIONAIRE MIX ▲   🍷

SERVES 1
1 measure rye whiskey
½ measure grenadine
½ measure curaçao
½ egg white
dash of Pernod

Shake the rye whiskey, grenadine, curaçao, and egg white together over ice cubes. Strain into a wine glass and, at the last minute, add a dash of Pernod.

CLOVER CLUB

SERVES 1
2 measures gin
1 measure lime juice
1 measure grenadine
1 egg white

*Pour the gin, lime juice, and grenadine over ice cubes.
Add the egg white and shake vigorously until well frosted.
Strain into a chilled cocktail glass.*

WHY NOT? ▸

SERVES 1
cracked ice
dash of lemon juice
2 measures gin
1 measure peach brandy
1 measure Noilly Prat vermouth
twist of lemon peel

*Put the cracked ice into a mixing glass and splash a little
lemon juice over them. Pour in the gin, peach brandy,
and Noilly Prat, and stir to mix. Strain the liquid into a
chilled cocktail glass. Serve with the twist of lemon peel.*

PLANTER'S TEA ◂

More refreshing, they say, than a cup of tea made the
British way. This one should really get you going.

SERVES 1
2 measures strong black tea
2 measures dark rum
1¼ cups orange juice
⅔ cup fresh lemon juice
orange slices
superfine sugar, to taste

*Mix the tea, dark rum, orange juice, and fresh lemon
juice together. Heat gently, sweeten to taste, and serve in
an Irish Coffee glass or mug with the slices of orange.*

ACADEMIA DA CACHAÇA

RIO DE JANEIRO

This modest Rio bar was mixing Caipirinhas long before the Brazilian drink became a global standard. Classy yet casual, the place is a revelation to those who think of a Caipirinha as a simple mixture of lime, sugar, ice, and the sugarcane rum cachaça. Indeed, it transpires there are many sorts of cachaça and you'll simply never find a greater range anywhere else. After more than 22 years in business, the Academia's Caipirinhas are still widely acknowledged as the best in Brazil. The "Academy" also mixes the spirit into other award-winning cocktails.

Beneath an unusual Brazilian flag ceiling decoration made from raffia, the bar showcases a private connoisseur's collection of

BEST FOR
Caipirinhas and cachaça

CAIPIRINHA ACADÊMICA

The signature Caipirinha Acadêmica is a cocktail of muddled citron, honey, and the artisanal cachaça brand, Seleta. Both the cocktail and Seleta, produced in the Brazilian state of Minas Gerais, have become bestsellers at the Academia da Cachaça.

SERVES 1

2 citrons (similar in appearance to a lemon, with a highly fragrant peel)
½ cup honey
3 measures Cachaça Seleta

Wash the citrons, cut them into pieces, and place them in a glass. Sprinkle with the honey and crush the citron pieces, pulp side up, with a pestle. (Academia da Cachaça has a long, wooden Brazilian one made specifically for this purpose.) Add the cachaça and stir to mix. Add ice cubes and stir again.

❖

"The key is to choose the right fruit, to squeeze, muddle, or crush it to get the most flavor, and then to concentrate on getting the quantities of cachaça, ice, and sugar just right."

Barman, Antonio Marcos

2,000 cachaça bottles, arranged thematically to present the drink's 130-year history. The drinks list is scarcely less generous, listing a hundred or so different regional cachaças, alongside spiced and fruit-infused varieties, the oldest bottle dating back to 1875. There are many artisanal brands, including Lua Cheia, a fruity golden liqueur. Passion fruit and coconut batida cocktails come with real fruit pieces and juice.

Partners Edméa Falcão, Renata Quinderé, and Hélcio Santos wanted cachaça to be taken seriously, and that's an aim they've certainly achieved. But the Academia is also a much-lauded restaurant, serving northeast Brazilian specialties. As you sample shredded beef with cassava cream puree and sip your drink, you have to reflect there's nothing better than returning to the source. And so it is with Caipirinhas.

ACADEMIA DA CACHAÇA
Rua Conde Bernadotte 26
(Loja G)
Leblon
CEP 22430–200
Rio de Janeiro
Brazil
+ 55 21 2529 2680
www.academiadacachaca.com.br

Open daily
12:00 noon until the last customer leaves

LOUNGING AROUND

In this day and age, none of us spend enough time in relaxation mode. However, when you do find time to sit by the pool, hang out with friends in the park, flick through a magazine on the couch, or snuffle through the afternoon movie, make sure you have one of these delicious cocktails beside you.

FROZEN MINT JULEP ‹   ☆ ▢

The precise origins of the Mint Julep are lost in the mists of time, but the cocktail was probably first made somewhere in the southern United States in the eighteenth century. This version is delicious.

SERVES 1
crushed ice
2 measures bourbon
1 measure lemon juice
1 measure sugar syrup
6 fresh mint leaves
fresh mint sprig

Put the crushed ice into a blender or food processor. Add the bourbon, lemon juice, sugar syrup, and fresh mint leaves, and blend at low speed until slushy. Pour into a chilled lowball glass and dress with the fresh mint sprig.

The word "julep" probably derives from the Arabic word *julab*, meaning "rosewater." A julep has been a sweet, medicinal drink since at least the fifteenth century. Today, the Mint Julep cocktail is regarded as the quintessential drink of the Deep South.

Mint Juleps are traditionally served in a special silver or pewter julep cup, which is held only by the bottom or top edges, to allow the condensation to turn to frost. A julep cup would be particularly suitable for this Frozen Mint Julep but if you don't have a suitable tankard at hand, a Collins glass, highball glass, or any tall glass will more than suffice. Use a good-quality bourbon or rye whiskey, and fresh mint is absolutely essential.

STAR DAISY ▶

A Daisy is a cocktail with a high proportion of alcohol that is sweetened with fruit syrup. Perhaps it gets its name from the now old-fashioned slang, when the word "daisy" referred to something exceptional and special.

SERVES 1
2 measures gin
1½ measures apple brandy
1½ measures lemon juice
1 teaspoon sugar syrup
½ teaspoon triple sec
club soda

Pour the gin, apple brandy, lemon juice, sugar syrup, and triple sec over ice cubes and shake vigorously. Strain into a chilled lowball glass and fill with club soda.

GIN SLINGER ◀

SERVES 1
1 teaspoon sugar
1 measure lemon juice
1 teaspoon water
2 measures gin
orange peel

Stir the sugar, lemon juice, and water together until the sugar has dissolved. Add the gin and stir again. Half-fill a chilled lowball glass with ice cubes and strain the cocktail over them. Cut the orange peel into a twist and pierce the straw with it, or use it to decorate the rim of the glass.

BRANDY CUBAN ▸

SERVES 1
1½ measures brandy
½ measure lime juice
cola
slice of lime

Pour the brandy and lime juice into a lowball glass half-filled with ice cubes. Fill with cola and stir gently. Decorate with the slice of lime.

CRANBERRY COLLINS

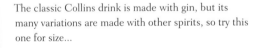

The classic Collins drink is made with gin, but its many variations are made with other spirits, so try this one for size...

SERVES 1
2 measures vodka
¾ measure elderflower cordial
3 measures white cranberry and apple juice
club soda
slice of lime

Shake the vodka, elderflower cordial, and white cranberry and apple juice over ice cubes until well frosted. Strain into a highball glass with more ice cubes and fill with club soda to taste. Dress with the slice of lime.

JAMAICA MULE ▸

SERVES 1
2 measures white rum
1 measure dark rum
1 measure golden rum
1 measure Falernum
1 measure lime juice
ginger beer
pineapple wedges
candied ginger

Shake the white, dark, and golden rums, Falernum, and lime juice vigorously over ice cubes until well frosted. Strain the mixture into a chilled highball glass and fill with ginger beer. Dress the drink with wedges of pineapple and chunks of candied ginger.

BLINKER ▲

SERVES 1
2 measures rye whiskey
2½ measures grapefruit juice
1 teaspoon grenadine

Shake the rye whiskey, grapefruit juice, and grenadine vigorously over ice cubes until well frosted. Strain into a chilled cocktail glass.

Falernum, which features in the Jamaica Mule, is a sweet, slightly alcoholic, fairly thick syrup, flavored with ginger, almonds, and lime, and sometimes cloves, allspice or vanilla. It's often used in tropical or Caribbean drinks.

GIN SLING COCKTAIL ◄

SERVES 1
large chunk of ice
juice of ¾ lemon
½ tablespoon powdered (confectioner's) sugar
1 measure gin
still water
slice of lemon
dash of Angostura bitters

Put the large chunk of ice, lemon juice, powdered sugar, and gin into a lowball glass. Fill with still water. Float the slice of lemon on top and add a dash of Angostura bitters.

RUM DAISY ◄

SERVES 1
2 measures golden rum
1 measure lemon juice
1 teaspoon sugar syrup
½ teaspoon grenadine
cracked ice
orange slice

Pour the golden rum, lemon juice, sugar syrup, and grenadine over ice cubes and shake until well frosted. Half-fill a chilled lowball glass with the cracked ice and strain the cocktail over it. Dress the drink with a slice of orange.

BANANA COLADA ◂

SERVES 1
4–6 ice cubes, crushed
2 measures white rum
4 measures pineapple juice
1 measure Malibu
1 banana, peeled and sliced
pineapple wedges

Mix the crushed ice in a blender with the white rum, pineapple juice, Malibu, and sliced banana. Blend until smooth, then, without straining, pour into a chilled highball glass and serve with pineapple wedges and a straw.

Long Island Iced Tea—originally just vodka with a dash of cola—dates back to the days of Prohibition, when it was drunk from teacups in an attempt to fool the Bureau of Alcohol, Tobacco, and Firearms' agents that it was iced tea.

LONG ISLAND ICED TEA

SERVES 1
2 measures vodka
1 measure gin
1 measure white tequila
1 measure white rum
½ measure white crème de menthe
2 measures lemon juice
1 teaspoon sugar syrup
cracked ice
cola
slice of lime or lemon

Shake the vodka, gin, tequila, rum, crème de menthe, lemon juice, and sugar syrup vigorously over ice cubes until well frosted. Strain into a highball glass filled with cracked ice and fill with cola. Dress with the lime or lemon slice.

BRANDY JULEP ◄

SERVES 1

cracked ice

2 measures brandy

1 teaspoon sugar syrup

4 fresh mint leaves

fresh mint sprig

slice of lemon

Fill a chilled lowball glass with cracked ice. Add the brandy, sugar syrup, and mint leaves, and stir well to mix. Decorate the cocktail with the sprig of fresh mint, the slice of lemon, and a straw.

If you leave out the pineapple juice and wedge from the Cuban Special, it becomes a Cuban Sidecar—but don't do it. The fruit turns it into a longer drink that's perfect for an afternoon in the sun.

CUBAN SPECIAL ▲

SERVES 1

2 measures rum

1 measure lime juice

1 tablespoon pineapple juice

1 teaspoon triple sec

pineapple wedge

Pour the rum, lime juice, pineapple juice, and triple sec over ice cubes and shake until well frosted. Strain into a chilled cocktail glass and dress with the wedge of pineapple.

ROYAL WEDDING ▲

SERVES 1
1 measure kirsch
1 measure peach brandy
1 measure orange juice

Shake the kirsch, peach brandy, and orange juice vigorously over ice cubes until well frosted. Strain into a chilled cocktail glass.

PALM BEACH ▲

If it's been a long time since your last vacation, conjure up the blue skies and rolling surf of Florida with this sunny cocktail.

SERVES 1
cracked ice
1 measure white rum
1 measure gin
1 measure pineapple juice
pineapple leaves

Shake the rum, gin, and pineapple juice vigorously over the cracked ice until well frosted. Pour into a chilled highball glass and decorate with the pineapple leaves.

JOCOSE JULEP ▾

SERVES 1
4–6 ice cubes, crushed
3 measures bourbon
1 measure green crème de menthe
1½ measures lime juice
1 teaspoon sugar syrup
5 fresh mint leaves
cracked ice
sparkling water
fresh mint sprig

Put the crushed ice into a blender or food processor, add the bourbon, green crème de menthe, lime juice, sugar syrup, and fresh mint leaves, and process until smooth. Fill a chilled lowball glass with the cracked ice and pour in the cocktail. Fill with sparkling water and stir gently to mix. Dress with a sprig of fresh mint.

It is said in Virginia that a julep, above all, is a state of mind. Considering that the word *jocose* means "merry"—you get the general idea of of the Jocose Julep from its name.

BIRD OF PARADISE COOLER

SERVES 1
2 measures gin
1 measure lemon juice
1 teaspoon grenadine
1 teaspoon sugar syrup
1 egg white
cracked ice
sparkling water

Vigorously shake the gin, lemon juice, grenadine, sugar syrup, and egg white over ice cubes until well frosted. Half-fill a chilled lowball glass with the cracked ice and pour the cocktail over it. Fill with the sparkling water.

AMBROSIA ◄

SERVES 1
1½ measures brandy
1½ measures applejack
½ teaspoon raspberry syrup
champagne, chilled
1 raspberry

Shake the brandy, applejack, and raspberry syrup vigorously over ice cubes until well frosted. Strain into a chilled wine glass. Fill with chilled champagne and dress with a raspberry.

PARADISE ►

SERVES 1
2 measures apricot brandy
1 measure gin
1½ measures orange juice
½ teaspoon grenadine

Shake the apricot brandy, gin, orange juice, and grenadine vigorously over ice cubes until well frosted. Strain into a chilled cocktail glass.

AMIGOS PIÑA COLADA ◄

SERVES 4
10–12 ice cubes, crushed
1 cup rum
1¼ cups pineapple juice
5 measures coconut cream
2 measures dark rum
2 measures light cream
pineapple wedges
cocktail cherries

Mix the crushed ice in a blender with the rum, pineapple juice, coconut cream, dark rum, and cream. Blend until smooth. Pour, without straining, into chilled lowball or hurricane glasses and decorate with the wedges of pineapple and cocktail cherries.

GRAND BAHAMA ►

SERVES 1
1 measure white rum
½ measure brandy
measure triple sec
1 measure lime juice
slice of lime

Shake the white rum, brandy, triple sec, and lime juice vigorously over ice cubes until well frosted. Strain into a chilled cocktail glass. Serve with the slice of lime.

The classic Piña Colada, invented in the 1950s in Puerto Rico, usually uses light rum, pineapple juice, and coconut cream. This version is stronger because it contains dark rum as well. The cream also makes it richer than the original.

CHICA CHICA ‹

SERVES 1
2 measures raspberry vodka
1 measure Chambéry (a type of white vermouth)
2 measures cranberry and raspberry juice
crushed ice
1 measure apple juice
lemon-flavored soda pop
apple slices

Mix the raspberry vodka, Chambéry, cranberry and raspberry juice, and crushed ice together in a chilled highball glass. Stir in the apple juice and fill with lemon-flavored soda pop to taste. Finish with the slices of apple.

It is easy to buy flavored vodkas, but you can make your own. Add a small quantity of the flavoring—a few raspberries, blueberries, dried apricots, a piece of lime or lemon peel or even a sliver of chile pepper— to a bottle of vodka and let stand for 12 hours.

There are many variations on the Zombie, generally a mixture of three types of rum and various fruity libations. The name of this exceptionally strong cocktail derives from its obvious effect on the consumer.

KLONDIKE COOLER ◄

You can, of course, make this with a favorite whiskey if you have one.

SERVES 1
½ teaspoon superfine sugar
1 measure ginger ale
cracked ice
2 measures blended whiskey
sparkling water
twist of lemon peel

Put the superfine sugar into a chilled highball glass and add the ginger ale. Stir until the sugar has dissolved, then fill the glass with cracked ice. Pour the whiskey over the ice and fill with the sparkling water. Stir gently to mix and dress with the twist of lemon peel.

WALKING ZOMBIE ▲

SERVES 1
1 measure white rum
1 measure golden rum
1 measure dark rum
1 measure apricot brandy
1 measure lime juice
1 measure pineapple juice
1 teaspoon sugar syrup
cracked ice
orange and lime slices

Pour the white, golden, and dark rum, apricot brandy, lime juice, pineapple juice, and sugar syrup over ice cubes. Shake vigorously until frosted. Half-fill a chilled highball glass with the cracked ice and strain the cocktail over it. Dress with the slices of orange and lime.

A.J. SHAKE ▶

As you'll realize from the list of ingredients, the "A.J." stands for applejack, but calvados will do just as well.

SERVES 1
1½ measures applejack
1 measure grapefruit juice

Shake the applejack and grapefruit juice vigorously over ice cubes until well frosted. Strain into a chilled cocktail glass.

SWEET SINGAPORE SLING ▲

SERVES 1
1 measure gin
2 measures cherry brandy
dash of lemon juice
cracked ice
club soda
cocktail cherry

Vigorously shake the gin, cherry brandy, and a dash of lemon juice over ice cubes until well frosted. Half-fill a chilled lowball glass with cracked ice and strain in the cocktail. Fill with club soda and decorate with the cocktail cherry.

The classic Singapore Sling is still served at the Raffles Hotel in Singapore, where it was invented by barman Ngiam Tong Boon in the early twentieth-century. The original contained Benedictine. The cherry brandy in this refreshing variant ensures the drink retains its trademark rosy pink hue.

ZOMBIE PRINCE ◀

SERVES 1

dash of Angostura bitters
1 measure white rum
1 measure golden rum
1 measure dark rum
½ measure lemon juice
½ measure orange juice
½ measure grapefruit juice
1 teaspoon brown sugar

Splash the Angostura bitters over ice cubes in a mixing glass, add the white rum, golden rum, dark rum, lemon juice, orange juice, and grapefruit juice, and add the brown sugar. Stir to mix well, then strain into a chilled highball glass.

SEX ON THE BEACH

Vacation drinks are often long and fruity and this refreshing cocktail is designed to make you reminisce over happy days in the sun.

SERVES 1

1 measure peach schnapps
1 measure vodka
2 measures fresh orange juice
3 measures cranberry and peach juice
crushed ice
squeeze of lemon juice
orange peel

Shake the peach schnapps, vodka, orange juice, and cranberry and peach juice over ice cubes until frosted. Strain into a highball glass filled with crushed ice and add a squeeze of lemon juice. Decorate with the orange peel.

WHITE LION ▲

SERVES 1

4–6 ice cubes, cracked
dash of Angostura bitters
dash of grenadine
2 measures white rum
1 measure lemon juice
1 teaspoon sugar syrup

Shake the cracked ice in a cocktail shaker with the Angostura bitters, grenadine, white rum, lemon juice, and sugar syrup until a frost forms. Strain into a chilled cocktail glass.

TEQUILA FIZZ ▸

A fizz usually contains liquor and at least one fruit juice, filled with soda pop. Fizzes are always shaken rather than mixed.

SERVES 1

3 measures white tequila
1 measure grenadine
1 measure lime juice
1 egg white
cracked ice
ginger ale

Shake the white tequila, grenadine, lime juice, and egg white vigorously over ice cubes until well frosted. Half-fill a chilled highball or lowball glass with cracked ice and strain the cocktail over it. Fill with ginger ale.

BELLE COLLINS

SERVES 1

3 fresh mint sprigs
4–6 ice cubes, crushed
2 measures gin
1 measure lemon juice
1 teaspoon sugar syrup
sparkling water

Crush two of the sprigs of fresh mint and place them in a chilled highball glass. Add the crushed ice and pour in the gin, lemon juice, and sugar syrup. Fill with sparkling water, stir gently, and decorate with the remaining mint sprig.

COUSIN COLLINS ▸

SERVES 1

2 measures applejack or calvados

1 measure lemon juice

½ teaspoon sugar syrup

crushed ice

dash of orange bitters

sparkling water

lemon slices

Blend the applejack or calvados, lemon juice, and sugar syrup with crushed ice and a dash of orange bitters at medium speed for ten seconds. Pour into a chilled lowball glass and fill with sparkling water. Stir gently and dress with the lemon slices.

MAGNA CARTA ▸

If you really want to lounge around in style, you can use champagne rather than sparkling wine to provide the finishing touches to this cocktail.

SERVES 1

lime wedge

superfine sugar

2 measures white tequila

1 measure triple sec

sparkling wine or champagne, chilled

Rub the rim of a wine or highball glass with the wedge of lime and then dip the glass in superfine sugar to frost it. Over ice cubes, stir the white tequila and triple sec together in a mixing glass. Strain into the prepared glass and fill with the chilled sparkling wine.

END OF THE ROAD ▸

SERVES 1

3 measures gin
1 measure crème de menthe
1 measure pastis
cracked ice
sprig of mint
club soda

Stir the gin, crème de menthe, and pastis together over ice cubes. Strain into a highball glass filled with the cracked ice and dress with a sprig of mint. Fill with club soda, unless you feel like a shorter drink.

SEABREEZE

Pink grapefruit juice is much sweeter and subtler than its paler cousin, so it's ideal for cocktails where you want just a slight sharpness.

SERVES 1

1½ measures vodka
½ measure cranberry juice
pink grapefruit juice

Shake the vodka and cranberry juice over ice cubes until frosted. Pour into a chilled highball glass and fill with pink grapefruit juice to taste.

COSTA DEL SOL ▸

SERVES 1

2 measures gin
1 measure apricot brandy
1 measure triple sec

Shake the gin, apricot brandy, and triple sec vigorously over ice cubes until well frosted. Strain into a chilled cocktail glass or lowball glass.

BLACK AND TAN ▸

SERVES 1

⅔ cup ginger ale, chilled
⅔ cup ginger beer, chilled
slice of lime

Pour the ginger ale into a chilled lowball glass, then add the ginger beer. Do not stir, but dress with the slice of lime.

FROZEN STRAWBERRY DAIQUIRI ◂ 🍸

SERVES 1

crushed ice
2 measures white rum
1 measure lime juice
1 teaspoon sugar syrup
7 strawberries

Mix the crushed ice in a blender and then add the white rum, lime juice, sugar syrup, and six of the strawberries. Blend until slushy. Pour the concoction into a chilled cocktail glass and dress with the remaining strawberry.

The British pub drink known as Black and Tan is a combination of light and dark beers. This lighter and more refreshing Black and Tan comes from the pairing of nonalcoholic pale-colored ginger ale with dark-colored ginger beer.

MIAMI BEACH ◄

SERVES 1

2 measures Scotch whisky

1½ measures dry vermouth

2 measures grapefruit juice

twist of orange peel

Shake the Scotch, dry vermouth, and grapefruit juice over ice cubes. Shake vigorously until well frosted, then strain into a chilled cocktail glass and serve with the twist of orange peel.

PALM BEACH SOUR

SERVES 1

⅓ measure gin

⅓ measure grapefruit juice

⅙ measure dry vermouth

2–3 drops Angostura bitters

1 teaspoon superfine sugar

1 egg white

Shake the gin, grapefruit juice, dry vermouth, Angostura bitters, sugar, and egg white with ice cubes. Strain into a chilled cocktail glass or wine glass.

HALLEY'S COMFORT ►

SERVES 1

cracked ice

2 measures Southern Comfort

2 measures peach schnapps

sparkling water

slice of lemon

Half-fill a chilled lowball glass or highball glass with the cracked ice. Pour the Southern Comfort and peach schnapps over the ice and fill with sparkling water. Stir gently and dress with the slice of lemon.

THE FLATIRON LOUNGE

NEW YORK CITY

Like a good cocktail, there are a number of ingredients that make a good bar. The Flatiron Lounge in New York City is a perfect example. Situated near the historic Flatiron Building (why not admire the architecture and then retire to the Lounge for a drink?), this bar has a cool Art Deco interior with dark red leatherette banquettes and cobalt blue mirrors. Opened in 2003, this classy joint marks a relaxed return to the luxurious abandon of the bygone classic cocktail era of the 1920s. The meticulously restored Art Deco bar was once leaned on by Frank Sinatra and the Rat Pack at New York's legendary Manhattan Ballroom.

But it's the cocktails that make this one of the world's best bars. It has a unique menu of modern, tasty cocktails that all contain the

BEST FOR
classic cocktails in Art Deco splendor

LONG ISLAND GREEN TEA

SERVES 4

1½ cup superfine sugar

½ cup hot water

1 cup fresh lemon juice

25 fl oz/750 ml bottle sake

10 green tea bags

⅓ cup premium gin

⅓ cup premium
   lemon vodka

4 teaspoons grenadine

8 brandied cherries

Make a sour mix by dissolving the sugar in the hot water. Add the lemon juice and chill. Warm the saké by immersing the bottle in hot water. Decant the sake into a bowl, add the tea bags, and steep for 40 minutes. Strain the sake mixture into a pitcher. Stir in the sour mix, gin, and vodka. Fill four tall glasses with ice cubes. Pour the mixture over the ice, adding one teaspoon of grenadine to each glass. Serve with two brandied cherries on a stick.

"A good cocktail should give you more than a buzz, it should lift you up and take you someplace else."

Julie Reiner, mixologist and co-owner of the Flatiron Lounge

perfect blend of alcohol and exotic fresh ingredients. These drinks are like art in a glass. The menu changes seasonally and there are usually specials, depending on what's available. The menu is truly unique and full of house specialty infusions, such as Harvest Punch (vodka steeped in Pacific Rim teas, flavored with passion flower and mint), or Juniper Breeze (a fresh mix of Plymouth gin, elderflower cordial, grapefruit, lime, and cranberry) and guest cocktails from the finest mixologists in the city.

In a city of a thousand bars (and more), this is a special place. The drinks come as they should—surprising, varied, fresh, full of flavor, and demanding to be sipped and savored. Tip: Try the "flight of the day," where you can have your tastebuds transported to anywhere in the world on board a trio of miniature cocktails served on a custom-made wooden tray.

FLATIRON LOUNGE

Flatiron Building

37 West 19th Street

(between 5th and 6th Avenue)

NY 10011

USA

(212) 727-7741

www.flatironlounge.com

Open daily

Sunday through Wednesday

5:00 p.m to 2:00 a.m.

Thursday, Friday, and Saturday

5:00 p.m. to 4:00 a.m.

BEFORE DINNER

Sometimes it's hard to know what to drink before you eat. You certainly don't want to approach dinner feeling bloated and sluggish. Indeed, an aperitif should sharpen your appetite, not kill it. So think carefully about what you order. Thankfully, however, if you decide to prime your palette, there is a cocktail here for you.

COSMOPOLITAN ◄

This fashionable cocktail, made famous by the TV show *Sex and the City*, is ideal before a sophisticated dinner party.

SERVES 1
2 measures vodka
1 measure triple sec
1 measure fresh lime juice
1 measure cranberry juice
twist of orange peel

Shake the vodka, triple sec, lime juice, and cranberry juice over ice cubes until well frosted. Strain into a chilled cocktail glass and dress with a twist of orange peel.

Although a relative newcomer to the scene, having arrived sometime in the mid-1980s, probably from Miami's fashionable South Beach, the Cosmopolitan (or Cosmo, as those who imbibe it frequently call it) has rapidly established itself as a classic cocktail.

In part, this may be due to its subsequent association with New York's Manhattan, but the Cosmopolitan is also ideal before a dinner party in slightly more humble surroundings.

In its initial incarnation, the cranberry juice was present to give the merest hint of pink, but most recipes now include a good dose of cranberry, which imparts a rich, almost ruby color, and gently undercuts the citrusy combination of the orange-flavored triple sec and the lime.

Whatever liquor it utilizes, the key ingredient of a Sour, as the name suggests, is citrus juice. Sours are usually served in a sour or a cocktail glass and garnished with a cocktail cherry, though on the rocks in a lowball glass will be fine.

ITALIAN STALLION ▾

SERVES 1
4–6 ice cubes
dash of Angostura bitters
2 measures bourbon
1 measure Campari
½ measure sweet vermouth
twist of lemon peel

Put the ice cubes into a mixing glass, add a dash of Angostura and pour in the bourbon, Campari, and sweet vermouth. Stir well to mix, then strain into a chilled cocktail glass and dress with the twist of lemon peel.

BOSTON SOUR ◂

SERVES 1
1 measure lemon or lime juice
2 measures blended Scotch whisky
1 egg white
1 teaspoon superfine sugar or sirop de gomme
lemon slice
cocktail cherry

Shake the lemon or lime juice, whisky, egg white, and sugar or syrup over ice cubes and strain into a cocktail glass or sour glass. Finish with the slice of lemon and a cocktail cherry.

BELLINITINI ▸

A delightful variation on one of the most well-known aperitifs—just peachy.

SERVES 1

2 measures vodka
1 measure peach schnapps
1 measure peach juice
champagne, chilled

Shake the vodka, peach schnapps, and peach juice vigorously over ice cubes until well frosted. Strain into a chilled wine glass or flute and fill with the chilled champagne.

BELLINI

This delicious concoction was created by Giuseppe Cipriani at Harry's Bar in Venice, around 1943.

SERVES 1

1 measure fresh peach juice made from lightly sweetened liquidized peaches
superfine sugar
3 measures champagne, chilled

Dip the rim of a chilled flute glass into some peach juice and then into the sugar to create a sugar-frosted effect. Set the glass aside to dry. Pour the peach juice into the flute, carefully fill with the champagne and stir gently.

APPLE MARTINI ▸

Very much a cocktail of the moment, the Apple Martini, also known as an Appletini, is smooth and easy to drink. Sour apple schnapps instead of ordinary apple schnapps will enhance the sharpness, as will a splash of lemon juice. If you have applesauce at hand, you can use that instead of the apple juice or substitute applejack to increase the alcohol content.

SERVES 1

cracked ice
1 measure vodka
1 measure apple schnapps
1 measure apple juice
2 thin slices of apple

Shake the vodka, apple schnapps, and apple juice over cracked ice until frosted. Strain into a chilled cocktail glass and dress with the slices of apple.

JUAN COLLINS ‹

Another member of the Collins family—this one may hail from down Mexico way.

SERVES 1
cracked ice
2 measures white tequila
1 measure lemon juice
1 teaspoon sugar syrup
sparkling mineral water
lemon slice

Half-fill a chilled highball glass with cracked ice and pour in the white tequila, lemon juice, and sugar syrup. Fill with sparkling mineral water and stir gently. Dress with the slice of lemon.

BACK TO THE FUTURE ‹

SERVES 1
2 measures gin
1 measure slivovitz
1 measure lemon juice
twist of lemon peel

Shake the gin, slivovitz, and lemon juice vigorously over ice cubes until well frosted. Strain into a chilled cocktail glass and serve with the twist of lemon peel.

DEPTH CHARGE

When an anise-based spirit such as Pernod is mixed with water it turns the water cloudy, but the same doesn't happen when it's mixed with other spirits—until the ice starts melting...

SERVES 1
1 measure gin
1 measure Lillet
2 dashes Pernod

Shake the gin, Lillet, and Pernod over ice cubes until well frosted, then strain into a chilled cocktail glass containing one or two ice cubes.

MOSCOW MULE ☆ ▯

The name of this cocktail derives from its principal ingredient, vodka, which comes from Russia, hence "Moscow," and has something of a kick, hence "Mule."

SERVES 1
2 measures vodka
1 measure lime juice
cracked ice
ginger beer
lime slice

Shake the vodka and lime juice vigorously over ice cubes until well frosted. Half-fill a chilled highball glass with cracked ice and strain the cocktail over it. Fill with the ginger beer and dress with the slice of lime.

The Moscow Mule was invented in the 1950s when a barman at the Cock 'n' Bull in Hollywood discovered he'd ordered too many crates of ginger beer. So he mixed it with vodka and inadvertently created a classic. The drink became so popular that it kicked off a craze for "white whiskey," as vodka was known at the time.

COLLEEN ▲ ⅄

SERVES 1
2 measures Irish whiskey
1 measure Irish Mist
1 measure triple sec
1 teaspoon lemon juice

Shake the Irish whiskey, Irish Mist, triple sec, and lemon juice vigorously over ice cubes until well frosted. Strain into a chilled cocktail glass.

MONTGOMERY ▲

SERVES 1
3 measures gin or vodka
1 teaspoon vermouth
olive or lemon zest

Take the gin or vodka and add the vermouth. Stir with ice cubes, strain into a chilled cocktail glass, and add an olive or a little lemon zest.

ROLLS-ROYCE ▲

SERVES 1
4–6 ice cubes
3 measures gin
1 measure dry vermouth
1 measure sweet vermouth
¼ teaspoon Benedictine

Put the ice cubes into a mixing glass. Pour the gin, dry vermouth, sweet vermouth, and Benedictine over them. Stir well to mix and then strain into a chilled cocktail glass.

BRANDY OLD FASHIONED ◂

SERVES 1
1 sugar cube
dash of Angostura bitters
1 teaspoon water
3 measures brandy
cracked ice
twist of lemon peel

Place the sugar cube in a small, chilled old-fashioned or lowball glass, and add the Angostura bitters and water. Mash with a spoon until the sugar has dissolved, then pour in the brandy and stir. Add the cracked ice and decorate with a twist of lemon peel.

The Old Fashioned is such a ubiquitous cocktail that a small, straight-sided glass or lowball glass is also known as an "old-fashioned" glass. This version of the cocktail is based on brandy, rather than bourbon or Scotch.

VICTORY ▴

SERVES 1
2 measures Pernod
1 measure grenadine
sparkling mineral water

Shake the Pernod and grenadine vigorously over ice cubes until well frosted. Strain into a chilled highball glass and fill with the sparkling mineral water.

ROSITA ▶

SERVES 1
4–6 ice cubes
2 measures Campari
2 measures white tequila
½ measure dry vermouth
½ measure sweet vermouth
twist of lime peel

Put the ice cubes into a mixing glass and pour the Campari, white tequila, and dry and sweet vermouths over them. Stir well to mix, then strain into a chilled lowball glass and dress with the twist of lime peel.

THE BENTLEY ▲

Champagne cocktails tend to get better and better the more you drink of them...

SERVES 1
½ measure cognac or brandy
½ measure peach liqueur, peach brandy, or schnapps
juice of 1 passion fruit, strained
1 ice cube
champagne, chilled

Mix the cognac, peach liqueur, and passion fruit juice gently together in a chilled highball glass. Add the single ice cube and slowly pour in the champagne to taste.

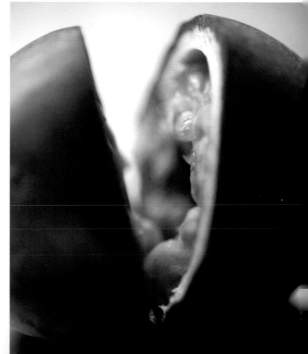

TNT ▶

SERVES 1

4–6 ice cubes, cracked

1 measure Pernod

1 measure rye whiskey

*Put the cracked ice into a mixing glass and pour the
Pernod and rye whiskey over it. Stir well to mix and strain
into a chilled cocktail glass.*

BRANDY SOUR ◀

First made in the Deep South in the mid-nineteenth
century, sours were based on brandy, but as distilled
French wines became harder to come by, bourbon or
rye replaced it as the spirit of choice. In this case, the
brandy has been reinstated.

SERVES 1

1 measure lemon or lime juice

2½ measures brandy

1 teaspoon superfine sugar or syrup de gomme

lemon or lime slice

maraschino cherry

*Shake the lemon or lime juice, brandy, and sugar or
syrup well over ice cubes and strain into a cocktail glass
or sour glass. Finish with a slice of lemon or lime and a
cocktail cherry.*

ORANGE GIN SLING

SERVES 1

2 measures gin

4 dashes orange bitters

*Pour the gin into a cocktail glass then carefully splash on
the orange bitters.*

DUCHESS ▾

SERVES 1
4–6 ice cubes, cracked
1 measure Pernod
1 measure sweet vermouth
1 measure dry vermouth

Put the cracked ice into a mixing glass. Pour the Pernod, sweet vermouth, and dry vermouth over it. Stir well to mix and then strain the mixture into a chilled cocktail glass or lowball glass.

GRAND DUCHESS ▴

SERVES 1
10 ice cubes, cracked
2 measures vodka
1 measure triple sec
3 measures cranberry juice
2 measures orange juice

Put half of the cracked ice into a mixing glass. Pour the vodka, triple sec, cranberry juice, and orange juice over the ice and stir well to mix. Half-fill a chilled lowball glass with the rest of the cracked ice and strain the cocktail over it.

ADAM 'N' EVE

SERVES 1

2 measures triple sec

1 measure vodka

1 measure grapefruit juice

1 measure cranberry juice

5–6 cubes pineapple

2 teaspoons superfine sugar

2 tablespoons crushed ice

strawberry slice

Shake the triple sec, vodka, grapefruit juice, and cranberry juice over ice cubes until well frosted, and strain the mixture into a chilled highball glass. In a blender, mix the pineapple with the sugar and the crushed ice until you have a frothy slush. Float this gently on the top of the cocktail and dress it with the slice of strawberry.

The base of the Adam 'n' Eve is sharp and astringent, while the top is sweet and frothy— it's a brilliant combination, but watch you don't lose your fig leaf.

WHISKEY COCKTAIL ▲

SERVES 1

2 measures bourbon

1 measure Southern Comfort

1 measure orange juice

dash of triple sec

orange slice

Shake the bourbon, Southern Comfort, orange juice, and a dash of triple sec vigorously over ice cubes until well frosted. Strain into a chilled cocktail glass and decorate with the slice of orange.

ALLIGATOR ◂

SERVES 1
2 measures vodka
1 measure Midori
½ measure dry vermouth
¼ teaspoon lemon juice
green melon balls

Pour the vodka, Midori, dry vermouth, and lemon juice over ice cubes and shake vigorously until well frosted. Strain into a chilled cocktail glass and serve with some green melon balls on a toothpick.

MIMOSA

This drink apparently acquired its name because it is the same color as the attractive yellow mimosa blossom.

SERVES 1
juice of 1 passion fruit
½ measure orange curaçao
crushed ice
champagne, chilled
slice of starfruit (carambola)
twist of orange peel

Scoop the passion fruit flesh into a pitcher or shaker and shake with the curaçao and a little crushed ice until frosted. Pour into the bottom of a champagne flute and fill with the champagne. Dress with the starfruit (carambola) and a twist of orange peel.

THIRD DEGREE ▸

SERVES 1
4–6 ice cubes, cracked
dash of Pernod
2 measures gin
1 measure dry vermouth
twist of lemon peel

Put cracked ice into a mixing glass. Splash the Pernod over the ice and pour in the gin and the dry vermouth. Stir well to mix, then strain into a chilled cocktail glass and serve with a twist of lemon peel.

STOCKHOLM

SERVES 1
1 sugar cube
2 measures lemon vodka
1 measure lemon juice
sparkling wine, chilled

Put the sugar cube in a wine glass with the lemon vodka and lemon juice. Stir to dissolve the sugar and fill with the chilled sparkling wine.

CHELSEA SIDECAR ▲

So strong are this cocktail's associations with the famous artists' and writers' hangout in New York that it's sometimes known as a Chelsea Hotel.

SERVES 1
2 measures gin
1 measure triple sec
1 measure lemon juice
twist of lemon peel

Pour the gin, triple sec, and lemon juice over ice cubes and shake vigorously until well frosted. Strain into a chilled cocktail glass and dress with the twist of lemon peel.

WEDDING BELLS ►

SERVES 1
4–6 ice cubes, cracked
dash of orange bitters
2 measures rye whiskey
1 measure triple sec
2 measures Lillet
twist of orange peel

Put the cracked ice into a mixing glass. Splash orange bitters over the ice and pour in the rye whiskey, triple sec, and Lillet. Stir well to mix, then strain into a chilled cocktail glass and serve with a twist of orange peel.

MANHATTAN ‹

It is thought that this drink originated at the Manhattan Club in New York City in the early 1870s, where it was invented for a banquet hosted by Jennie Jerome (mother of British prime minister Winston Churchill) in honor of presidential candidate Samuel J. Tilden.

SERVES 1
cracked ice
dash of Angostura bitters
3 measures rye whiskey
1 measure sweet vermouth
cocktail cherry

In a mixing glass, stir the Angostura bitters, whiskey, and vermouth together over cracked ice and mix well. Strain into a chilled cocktail glass or lowball glass and decorate with the cherry.

In the movie *Some Like it Hot,* starring Marilyn Monroe and Jack Lemmon, the girls throw an impromptu party on the train during which they pool their smuggled bootleg liquor to make Manhattans. They mention using bourbon whiskey rather than Canadian, and mix the cocktail in a hot water bottle.

TIGER BY THE TAIL ▲

SERVES 1
2 measures Pernod
4 measures orange juice
¼ teaspoon triple sec
crushed ice
twist of lime peel

Blend the Pernod, orange juice, and triple sec with the crushed ice until smooth. Pour into a chilled wine glass and dress with the twist of lime peel.

BOURBON SOUR ▾

Sours, which can be made with vodka, gin, or other spirits, as well as brandy and whiskey, are always shaken and should be served in a special sour glass, although if you don't have one, a highball or old-fashioned glass works equally well.

SERVES 1
1 measure lemon or lime juice
2 measures bourbon
1 teaspoon superfine sugar or syrup de gomme
orange slice

Shake the lemon or lime juice, bourbon, and sugar or syrup well over ice cubes and strain into a cocktail glass or sour glass. Finish with the slice of orange.

WHITE LADY

Simple, elegant, subtle, and much more powerful than its appearance may suggest, this is the perfect cocktail to serve before an al fresco summer dinner.

SERVES 1
cracked ice
2 measures gin
1 measure triple sec
1 measure lemon juice

Shake the gin, triple sec, and lemon juice vigorously over the cracked ice until well frosted. Strain into a chilled cocktail glass.

SAPPHIRE MARTINI ▸

SERVES 1
4–6 ice cubes, cracked
2 measures gin
½ measure blue curaçao
cocktail cherry

Put the cracked ice into a mixing glass and pour the gin and blue curaçao over it. Stir well to mix then strain into a chilled cocktail glass. Decorate with the cocktail cherry.

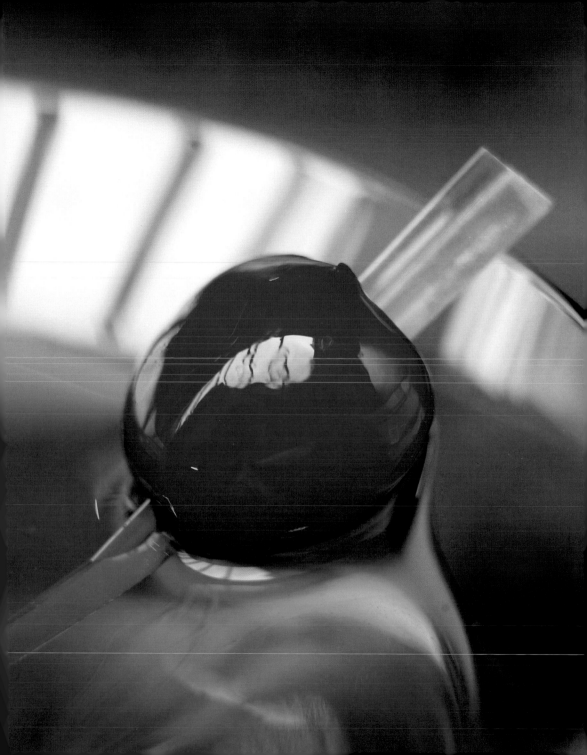

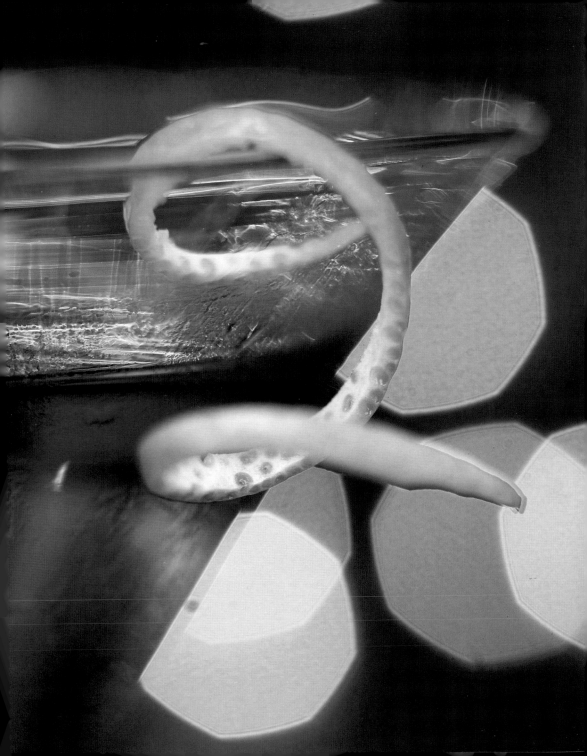

TOPAZ MARTINI ◄   ♈

SERVES 1

4–6 ice cubes, cracked

2 measures gin

½ measure orange curaçao

lemon slice

twist of orange or lemon peel

Put the cracked ice into a mixing glass and pour the gin and orange curaçao over it. Stir well to mix then strain into a chilled cocktail glass. Dress with the twist of orange or lemon peel.

KIR   ☆ ♉

SERVES 1

½ teaspoon crème de cassis

dry white wine, chilled

twist of lemon peel

Pour the the crème de cassis into a chilled wine glass and fill with the wine. Stir well, run the twist of lemon peel around the rim of the glass, squeeze, and drop it in.

LONDON FRENCH 75 ▲   ♉

The classic French 75 cocktail can be made with various liquors, but it is always filled with champagne. This version uses London gin.

SERVES 1

2 measures London gin

1 measure lemon juice

champagne, chilled

Shake the gin and lemon juice vigorously over ice cubes until well frosted. Strain into a chilled wine glass and fill with the chilled champagne. If you want to make it look fancier you can decorate it with a cocktail cherry.

GRAND ROYAL CLOVER CLUB ▸ 🍸

SERVES 1
2 measures gin
1 measure lemon juice
1 measure grenadine
1 egg white
twist of lemon peel

Pour the gin, lemon juice, grenadine, and egg white over ice cubes. Shake vigorously until well frosted. Strain into a chilled cocktail glass and serve with a twist of lemon peel.

CORDLESS SCREWDRIVER ▴

A shorter, shooter-style version of the famous Screwdriver (page 296), this gives an instant buzz.

SERVES 1
2 measures vodka, chilled
orange wedge
superfine sugar

Pour the chilled vodka into a shot glass. Dip a wedge of orange into the superfine sugar. Down the vodka in one gulp and suck on the orange.

Groucho Marx is well-known for claiming that he wouldn't want to belong to any club that was prepared to accept him as a member. The Grand Royal Clover Club is unlikely to have any shortage of willing members.

CITY SPACE BAR

MOSCOW

Many visitors arrive in the Russian capital without appreciating how colossal it is. It's one thing to know that this is Europe's largest city by far, but it's another matter entirely to clap eyes on it. Yet up here on the 34th floor of the tastefully minimalist Swissôtel Krasne Holmy, the world's most gaudily excessive, exciting, monolithic, gridlocked, enigmatic, chaotic, go-ahead, and contradictory metropolis is laid out sprawling at your feet.

Leaving rivals like the 25th-floor Sky Lounge and 27-story Red Bar in the shade, the central City Space Bar is now the place to come to watch the sunset—only temporarily—on the resurgent Russian empire. City Space offers a truly panoramic 360-degree view that

BEST FOR
watching the sun set

ISAEV

This is a Russian version of the classic James Bond vodka martini. Devised by City Space Bar's award-winning bartender and consultant mixologist, Alexander Kan, it is named for a famous Russian spy, Maxim Isaev (code name Shtirlitz), who worked in Germany during World War II. The drink distinguishes itself by replacing the standard ingredient of dry vermouth with birch juice. Although nowadays valued for its detoxifying effects, birch juice, made from silver birch trees, is a traditional and widely available Russian specialty. The premium juice served at the City Space Bar is freshly distilled in-house.

SERVES 1

2 measures vodka

1 measure birch juice

twist of lemon

Shake vodka and birch juice together with ice cubes in a mixing glass. Strain into a chilled cocktail glass. Garnish with a twist of lemon.

"Although we aim to deliver unique concoctions of flavors, a successful bar also has to deliver excellent customer service."

Manager, Bek Narzibekov

includes the Kremlin, St. Basil's Cathedral, the Moskva River, the resurrected Church of Christ the Savior, and the endless Moscow suburbs.

The entrance to the bar is dramatic too. Guests emerge from the elevator on the 33rd floor and rise into the middle of the bar's space-age glass bowl via a black spiral staircase. Here they're in a heady world, with a cocktail list presided over by manager Bek Narzibekov, who was part of the team at London's fabled Milk & Honey when it was named Best UK Bar. A honeyed Bloody Mary is just one of the innovative specialties available.

This being Moscow as it goes through its hottest-city-on-the-planet phase, footing the bill is also a breathtaking experience, but a trip to the Russian capital just wouldn't be complete without saying "na zdarovye" here.

CITY SPACE BAR

Kosmodamianskaya Naberezhnaya 52

Building 6

115054 Moscow

Russia

+7 495 787 9800

www.swissotel.com/moscow

Open daily

7:00 p.m. through 3:00 a.m.

IN THE MOOD

Any time, any place, anywhere—the words of the old Martini advertising slogan can't really be bettered. And for those immutable moments when you just must have a drink, when you need to stimulate your senses and tantalize your taste buds, here's an exemplary selection of classic and contemporary cocktails.

THE ULTIMATE CLASSIC MARTINI ◄   ☆ Ⓨ

Where to begin? For many, this is the ultimate mixed drink. More words have been written about the Martini than about any other cocktail.

SERVES 1
cracked ice
3 measures vodka or gin
1 teaspoon dry vermouth or to taste
green cocktail olive

Shake the vodka or gin and vermouth over cracked ice until well frosted. Strain into a chilled martini or cocktail glass and dress with the cocktail olive.

The simple fact is that the drink does not get its name from the popular Italian brand of vermouth. It may have been named for the city of Martinez, California, which claims to be the drink's birthplace, or after would-be inventor Martini di Arma di Taggia, who was a New York hotel barman. No one is completely sure. What is certainly true, however, is that the Martini was originally made with gin, but is now more often than not made with vodka.

Whichever spirit you use, though, make sure it is ice-cold, and chill the glass—obviously a Martini glass with its flared cup and elegant stem—too.

There are multitudinous variations on the basic Martini theme, some of which are featured elsewhere in this book.

In the mood

THE MODERN MARTINI ▾

Other good fruits to try with this recipe are kiwi, cranberry, pear, and watermelon.

SERVES 1
1 very ripe pomegranate
2 measures vodka or gin
dash of sugar syrup

Spoon the flesh of the pomegranate into a shaker and lightly crush or muddle. Add the vodka or gin and sugar syrup, and shake well over ice cubes. Strain into an iced martini or cocktail glass.

DIRTY MARTINI ▲

SERVES 1
3 measures gin
1 measure dry vermouth
½ measure brine from a jar of cocktail olives
cocktail olive

Vigorously shake the gin, dry vermouth, and cocktail olive brine over ice cubes until well frosted. Strain into a chilled martini or cocktail glass and dress with the cocktail olive.

THE LEGEND MARTINI

SERVES 1
2 measures vodka, iced
1 measure blackberry liqueur
1 measure fresh lime juice
dash of sugar syrup

Shake the iced vodka, blackberry liqueur, fresh lime juice, and a dash of sugar syrup together over ice cubes until really well frosted. Strain into an iced martini or cocktail glass.

RUM COCKTAIL ▲

SERVES 1
1 measure white rum
1 measure dark rum
1 measure Kahlúa
1 teaspoon lemon juice
2 teaspoon orange juice
lime slice

Vigorously shake the white rum, dark rum, Kahlúa, lemon juice, and orange juice over ice cubes until well frosted. Strain into a chilled lowball glass. Decorate with the slice of lime.

TOM COLLINS

Although invented in London in the early 1800s by a man called John Collins, this celebrated cocktail was commonly made with Old Tom gin and hence its name changed over time to Tom Collins.

SERVES 1
3 measures gin
2 measures lemon juice
½ measure sugar syrup
club soda
lemon slice

Shake the gin, lemon juice and sugar syrup vigorously over ice cubes until well frosted. Strain into a chilled highball glass, fill with the club soda, and dress with the slice of lemon.

BELLINI MARTINI ▶

SERVES 1
1 measure gin
½ measure brandy
½ measure peach puree
splash of sweet vermouth
peach slice

*Shake the gin, brandy, peach puree, and sweet
vermouth over ice cubes until well frosted. Strain into
an iced martini or cocktail glass and dress with the
slice of peach.*

FIFTY FIFTY ▲

This is the original version of the Martini, using equal
measures of gin and vermouth.

SERVES 1
1 measure gin
1 measure dry vermouth
cocktail olive

*Shake the gin and dry vermouth over ice cubes until
well frosted. Strain into a chilled cocktail glass. Drop in
a cocktail olive and serve.*

SILVER BERRY

This drink is perfect for a special occasion, although
you really can't drink very many.

SERVES 1
1 measure raspberry vodka, iced
1 measure crème de cassis, iced
1 measure Cointreau, iced
edible silver paper or frozen berry

*Carefully and slowly layer the vodka, crème de cassis,
and Cointreau, in that order, into a well-iced shot glass or
tall thin cocktail glass. The alcohol must be well iced first
and may need time to settle into their layers. Dress with
the silver paper or frozen berry.*

DAIQUIRI ☆ 🍸

Daiquiri is a town in Cuba, where this drink was said to have been invented in the early part of the twentieth century.

SERVES 1
cracked ice
2 measures white rum
¾ measure lime juice
½ teaspoon sugar syrup

Pour the rum, lime juice, and sugar syrup over cracked ice and shake vigorously until well frosted. Strain into a chilled cocktail glass.

GOLDEN FROG 🍸

Classic vodka cocktails were often intended to provide an alcoholic drink with no telltale signs on the breath, so they were usually fairly simple mixes of nonalcoholic flavors. Contemporary vodka cocktails, however, often include other liquors.

SERVES 1
4–6 ice cubes
1 measure vodka
1 measure Strega
1 measure Galliano
1 measure lemon juice

Whizz the ice cubes in a blender with the vodka, Strega, Galliano, and lemon juice. Blend until slushy and pour into a chilled cocktail glass.

GIBSON ▸

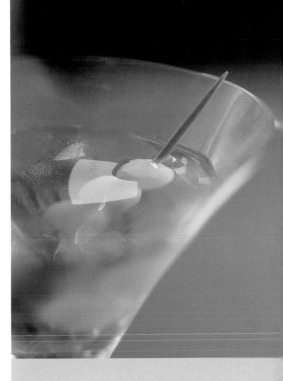

☆ 🍸

SERVES 1
cracked ice
3 measures gin
1 teaspoon dry vermouth
2–3 cocktail onions

Put the cracked ice into a mixing glass, pour the gin and vermouth over it, and stir well to mix. Strain into a chilled cocktail glass and dress with the cocktail onions.

HAWAIIAN ORANGE BLOSSOM ◂ 🍷

SERVES 1
2 measures gin
1 measure triple sec
2 measures fresh orange juice
1 measure pineapple juice
pineapple wedge and leaf

Vigorously shake the gin, triple sec, orange juice, and pineapple juice over ice cubes until well frosted. Strain into a chilled wine glass. Serve dressed with the pineapple wedge and leaf.

There are competing stories about the invention of the Gibson, but it was probably first made in the 1940s, at Manhattan's Players Club, for the artist Charles Dana Gibson. The key ingredient is the cocktail onions.

FAIR LADY ▸

SERVES 1
2 measures gin
1 measure orange juice
1 measure lime juice
1 egg white
dash of strawberry liqueur
1 strawberry
twist of lime peel

Vigorously shake the gin, orange juice, lime juice, egg white, and strawberry liqueur over ice cubes until well frosted. Strain into a chilled cocktail glass. Serve with a slice of the strawberry and the twist of lime peel.

BLUE BIRD ▲

SERVES 1
cracked ice
3 measures gin
1 measure blue curaçao
dash of Angostura bitters

Vigorously shake the gin, blue curaçao, and Angostura bitters over cracked ice until well frosted. Strain into a chilled cocktail or wine glass.

HARVEY WALLBANGER

This well-known contemporary classic cocktail is great at parties—and at any other time, too.

SERVES 1
3 measures vodka
8 measures orange juice
2 teaspoons Galliano
cherry
orange slice

Half-fill a highball glass with ice cubes, pour the vodka and orange over the ice, and float the Galliano on top. Garnish with the cherry and slice of orange. For a warming variant, mix a splash of ginger wine with the vodka and orange.

POLYNESIAN SOUR ◄

SERVES 1
4–6 ice cubes, crushed
2 measures light rum
½ measure guava juice
½ measure lemon juice
½ measure orange juice

Mix the crushed ice in a blender with the light rum, guava juice, lemon juice, and orange juice until smooth. Pour the mixture into a chilled cocktail glass.

MINT JULEP

The Mint Julep is the traditional drink of the Kentucky Derby, the horse race that has been held annually in Louisville, Kentucky, since 1875.

SERVES 1
2 fresh mint sprigs
1 tablespoon sugar syrup
crushed ice
3 measures bourbon whiskey

Put the leaves of one sprig of fresh mint and the sugar syrup into a chilled highball glass and mash with a teaspoon. Add crushed ice to fill the glass, then add the bourbon. Decorate with the other sprig of mint.

SAKETINI ◄

SERVES 1
3 measures gin
½ measure sake
twist of lemon peel

Vigorously shake the gin and sake over ice cubes until well frosted. Strain into a chilled cocktail glass and dress with the twist of lemon peel.

MANHATTAN DRY 🍸

This is a slightly sharper version of the classic Manhattan (page 171), using dry rather than sweet vermouth and curaçao.

SERVES 1
cracked ice
dash of Angostura bitters
3 measures rye whiskey
1 measure dry vermouth
2 dashes curaçao
cocktail cherry

Stir the liquids over cracked ice in a mixing glass and mix well. Strain into a chilled cocktail glass and decorate with the cherry.

There are a number of other versions of the Manhattan, including a Womanhattan, which comprises 1 measure of grenadine with 2 measures of rye whiskey, served with a twist of lemon peel.

PEACH DAIQUIRI ▲ 🔲 🍷

SERVES 1
2 measures white rum
1 measure lime juice
½ teaspoon sugar syrup
½ peach, peeled, pitted, and chopped

Blend the white rum, lime juice, sugar syrup, and chopped peach until smooth, then pour, without straining, into a chilled wine glass or lowball glass.

STREGA SOUR ▲ 𝒴

SERVES 1
2 measures gin
1 measure Strega
1 measure lemon juice
lemon slice

Shake the gin, Strega, and lemon juice vigorously over ice cubes until well frosted. Strain into a cocktail glass and decorate with the slice of lemon.

BOSTON SIDECAR ▲ 𝒴

SERVES 1
1½ measures white rum
½ measure brandy
½ measure triple sec
½ measure lemon juice
twist of orange peel

Pour the white rum, brandy, triple sec, and lemon juice over ice cubes and shake vigorously until well frosted. Strain into a chilled cocktail glass and decorate with the twist of orange peel.

RACQUET CLUB ◂

SERVES 1

dash of orange bitters

1 measure gin

1 measure dry vermouth

twist of orange peel

Dash the orange bitters over ice cubes in a mixing glass and pour in the gin and dry vermouth. Stir well to mix, then strain into a chilled cocktail glass. Serve with a twist of orange peel.

METROPOLITAN

SERVES 1

lemon wedge

1 tablespoon superfine sugar

cracked ice

½ measure vodka or lemon vodka

½ measure framboise or other
   raspberry liqueur

½ measure cranberry juice

½ measure orange juice

2 cranberries

Rub the outside rim of a cocktail glass with the lemon and dip the rim of the glass into the sugar to frost. Set aside. Put the cracked ice into a cocktail shaker and pour in the vodka, liqueur, cranberry juice, and orange juice. Shake vigorously for 10–20 seconds. Strain into the chilled glass, being careful not to disturb the frosting, and decorate with the cranberries.

SHADY LADY ▴

SERVES 1

3 measures tequila

1 measure applejack

1 measure cranberry juice

dash of lime juice

Shake the tequila, applejack, cranberry juice, and a dash of lime juice over ice cubes until well frosted. Strain into a chilled cocktail glass.

MULE'S HIND LEG ›

SERVES 1
½ measure apricot brandy
½ measure applejack
½ measure Benedictine
½ measure gin
½ measure maple syrup

*Vigorously shake the apricot brandy, applejack,
Benedictine, gin, and maple syrup over ice cubes until
well frosted. Strain into a chilled cocktail glass.*

CHAMPAGNE COCKTAIL ›

The classic champagne cocktail can be too sweet for
some people, so you can leave out the sugar because
it is the brandy that gives the treat and the kick.

SERVES 1
1 sugar cube
2 dashes of Angostura bitters
1 measure brandy
champagne, chilled

*Place the sugar cube with the drops of bitters in the
bottom of a chilled flute. Pour on the brandy and top
up slowly with champagne.*

MOJITO

The rum in this cocktail, which was allegedly a favorite of writer Ernest Hemingway, is rich in flavor and redolent of sunny vacation memories.

SERVES 1

1 teaspoon sugar
7 mint leaves
juice of ½ a lime
crushed ice
2 measures light rum
club soda

Put the sugar, six mint leaves, and the lime juice in a highball glass and crush or muddle the mint. Add the crushed ice and rum, then fill with the club soda. Finish with the remaining mint leaf.

PLANTER'S COCKTAIL ▲

SERVES 1

1 measure rum
juice of ½ a lime
1 teaspoon sugar syrup
dash of Angostura bitters

Mix the rum with the lime juice and sugar syrup and add a dash of Angostura bitters. Serve in a cocktail glass or lowball glass.

DEAUVILLE PASSION

Deauville was elegant, extravagant, and very fashionable resort on the Normandy coast of France during the 1920s and no doubt many great cocktails were created there.

SERVES 1

1¾ measures cognac
1¼ measures apricot curaçao
1¼ measures passion fruit juice
bitter lemon soda
mint leaves

Shake the cognac, apricot curaçao, and passion fruit juice over ice cubes until well frosted. Strain into a chilled highball glass, fill with the bitter lemon soda and dress with the mint leaves.

LOUNGE LIZARD ◄

SERVES 1
cracked ice
2 measures dark rum
1 measure amaretto
cola

*Half-fill a chilled highball glass with cracked ice and pour
the dark rum and amaretto over the ice. Fill with the cola
and stir gently.*

PINK SHERBET ROYALE

This is perfect for very special occasions on hot days
or after dinner watching a warm sun setting slowly.

SERVES 2
1¼ cups sparkling white wine, chilled
2 measures crème de cassis
1 measure brandy
1 scoop crushed ice
blackberries

*Mix half the wine in a blender with the crème de cassis,
brandy, and crushed ice until really frothy and frosted
(be careful it doesn't bubble over). Slowly whisk in a little
more wine and pour into frosted highball glasses. Top
with a few blackberries.*

BLANCHE ◄

SERVES 1

1 measure Pernod

1 measure triple sec

½ measure clear curaçao

Shake the Pernod, triple sec, and clear curaçao vigorously over ice cubes until well frosted. Strain into a chilled cocktail glass.

VODKATINI

A certain Mr. Bond popularized the use of vodka, rather than gin, as the base for a Martini, hence the Vodkatini is now widely accepted as a stylish and delicious alternative.

SERVES 1

1 measure vodka

dash of dry vermouth

lemon peel or olive

Pour the vodka over a handful of ice cubes in a mixing glass. Add the vermouth, stir well, and strain into a cocktail glass. Dress with the lemon peel or olive.

RAFFLES KNOCKOUT ▲

SERVES 1

1 measure triple sec

1 measure kirsch

dash of lemon juice

cocktail cherries

lemon slice

Vigorously shake the triple sec, kirsch, and lemon juice over ice cubes until well frosted. Strain into a chilled cocktail glass. Serve with a few cocktail cherries and the lemon slice.

BIRD OF PARADISO ⌄

SERVES 1
cracked ice
1½ measures white tequila
½ measure white crème de cacao
½ measure Galliano
1 measure orange juice
½ measure light cream
lemon wedges

Vigorously shake the white tequila, white crème de cacao, Galliano, orange juice, and light cream over cracked ice until well frosted. Strain into a chilled wine glass. Serve with some lemon wedges on a toothpick.

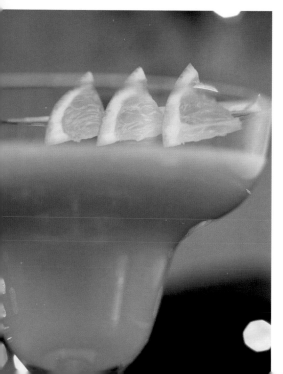

DERBY DAIQUIRI ▸

SERVES 1
4–6 ice cubes
2 measures white rum
1 measure orange juice
½ measure triple sec
½ measure lime juice
twist of lime peel

Mix the ice cubes, white rum, orange juice, triple sec, and lime juice in a blender until smooth, then pour, without straining, into a chilled cocktail glass. Serve with a twist of lime peel.

FLIRTINI

This combination of vodka and champagne is guaranteed to bring a sparkle to the eyes and a smile to the lips—what could be more attractive?

SERVES 1
¼ slice fresh pineapple, chopped
½ measure Cointreau, chilled
½ measure vodka, chilled
1 measure pineapple juice, chilled
champagne or sparkling white wine, chilled

Put the pineapple and Cointreau into a mixing glass or jug and muddle with a spoon to crush the pineapple. Add the vodka and pineapple juice and stir well, then strain into a champagne flute. Fill with champagne, although sparkling white wine works well too.

The Mai Tai was created in 1944 by Californian restaurateur Victor Bergeron, known as Trader Vic, for friends visiting from Tahiti. On tasting the drink they allegedly cried out "Mai Tai—Roe Ae," meaning "out of this world."

MAI TAI ◄

SERVES 1
cracked ice
2 measures white rum
2 measures dark rum
1 measure orange curaçao
1 measure lime juice
1 tablespoon orgeat syrup
1 tablespoon grenadine
cocktail cherries
pineapple slices
fruit peel

Shake the white and dark rums, curaçao, lime juice, orgeat syrup and grenadine vigorously over cracked ice until well frosted. Strain into a chilled cocktail glass and decorate flamboyantly with the cocktail cherries, pineapple slices and any other twists of fruit peel you have at hand.

DER RAUM

MELBOURNE

Some places are just ahead of the game and Melbourne's Der Raum is obviously one of them. The judges at the Australian Gourmet Traveler awards felt confident enough to name it 2008 Bar of the Year and *National Geographic* magazine has also given it the nod as one of the world's best drinking establishments.

Despite the German name (meaning "the room"), this is no thigh-slapping Bavarian beerhall. Rather it's a dark bare-boards bar on a slightly scruffy Richmond street that takes drinking very seriously indeed. Der Raum isn't the first place to pride itself on its impeccable use of fresh fruit juices, although it hand-squeezes them daily. But where else can one boast of owning the world's best

BEST FOR

serious drinking

PHARMACY

This is Matthew Bax's tribute to artist Damien Hirst.

SERVES 1

1 red chile pepper
1 pear, peeled and diced
½ lemon, chopped into pieces
3 tablespoons Plymouth gin
4 teaspoons honey water
    (2 teaspoons premium
    honey plus boiling bottled
    spring water)
large chunk of ice
medical jar
1 piece of sherbet or small
    sherbet candy
large syringe
2 teaspoons Aperol (an Italian
    liqueur)
steel medical tray

Roast the chile pepper over a flame. Wrap it in plastic wrap, wait 15 minutes, then scrape off the skin. In a mixing glass, add the pepper and pear to the gin. Cover, refrigerate, and let infuse for a few days. When you're ready to serve it, muddle the pieces of lemon in another mixing glass and then add the pepper, pear, gin, and honey water. Shake with a large chunk of ice and strain into the frozen medical jar. Fill the syringe with the Aperol. To serve, place the medical jar, syringe, and sherbet "pill" on the medical tray. To drink, inject the Aperol into the drink and drop in the sherbet.

"What you think is your most original idea, you'll always find in some old book, where even if the recipe's not exact, someone's had the same thought processes."

Owner, Matthew Bax

cocktail ice-making machine, which produces "the largest cube you've ever had the pleasure to drink with?" Apparently, the bigger the cube, the slower it cools your drink.

Der Raum is at the forefront of the new trend for "molecular mixology." This approach to cocktails is similar to the "molecular gastronomy" practiced by British celebrity chef Heston Blumenthal at the Fat Duck in Bray, England. By studying the science of taste, Der Raum's owner and executive bartender, Matthew Bax, has certainly taken a leaf from the famous chef's book.

On Thursday nights the bartenders run a "test lab" where they experiment with new mixtures, but every evening customers are treated to a spectacular sight behind the bar, where hundreds of spirit bottles hang from the ceiling by elastic straps, like a dense, swaying forest, all within the staff's easy reach.

DER RAUM
438 Church Street
Richmond
3121 Melbourne
Victoria
Australia
+61 3 9428 0055
www.derraum.com.au

Open Tuesday through Saturday
5:30 p.m. to 1:00 a.m.

KEEPING A CLEAR HEAD

Maybe you're watching your alcohol intake or recovering from an earlier session. Perhaps you're the designated driver or not yet of legal drinking age. Either way, you'll find that this selection of nonalcoholic cocktails—or "mocktails"—can be just as interesting and delicious as alcoholic ones.

SHIRLEY TEMPLE ◄ ☆ ▯

SERVES 1
2 measures lemon juice
½ measure grenadine
½ measure sugar syrup
cracked ice
ginger ale
orange slice

Shake the lemon juice, grenadine, and sugar syrup vigorously over ice cubes until well frosted. Half-fill a small, chilled highball glass with cracked ice and strain the liquid into it. Fill with ginger ale and dress with a slice of orange.

With her blonde ringlets, tap-dancing prowess, and affecting ability to portray orphans, Shirley Temple was an enormous box-office draw in the 1930s. When the pint-sized actress attended premieres and parties with adult movie stars, however, she was unfortunately too young to have whatever it was they were having. As a consequence, a thoughtful bartender mixed the original kiddie cocktail especially for her.

When she grew up, and became Shirley Temple Black, she also became a respected U.S. diplomat. When asked to comment on the drink, Temple allegedly said she didn't like it, because it's too sweet and she never made a cent out of the use of her name.

CITRUS FIZZ

This clever and refreshing variation on the classic Buck's Fizz is perfect for all the family.

SERVES 1
2 measures fresh orange juice, chilled
superfine sugar
a squeeze of lime juice
a few drops of Angostura bitters
2–3 measures sparkling water, chilled

Dip the rim of a flute into the orange juice and then into the superfine sugar. Stir together the rest of the orange juice, the lime juice, and the bitters and then pour the liquid into the glass. Fill with water to taste.

RANCH GIRL ▸

SERVES 1
1 measure lime juice
1 measure barbecue sauce
Worcestershire sauce
Tabasco sauce
tomato juice
lime slices
1 pickled jalapeño pepper

Shake the lime juice, barbecue sauce, and dashes of Worcestershire and Tabasco sauce over ice cubes until well frosted. Pour into a chilled highball glass, fill with tomato juice, and stir. Dress with a couple of slices of lime and a pickled jalapeño pepper.

BABY BELLINI ▸

SERVES 1
2 measures peach juice
1 measure lemon juice
sparkling apple juice

Pour the peach juice and lemon juice into a chilled champagne flute and stir well. Fill with sparkling apple juice and stir again.

BITE OF THE APPLE ▲

SERVES 1

crushed ice

5 measures apple juice

1 measure lime juice

½ teaspoon orgeat syrup

1 tablespoon applesauce or apple puree

Dash of cinnamon

*Mix the crushed ice in a blender with the apple
juice, lime juice, orgeat syrup, and applesauce until
smooth. Pour into a chilled lowball glass and sprinkle
with cinnamon.*

BRIGHT GREEN COOLER ▲

SERVES 1

3 measures pineapple juice

2 measures lime juice

1 measure green peppermint syrup

cracked ice

ginger ale

twist of cucumber

lime slice

*Shake the pineapple juice, lime juice, and green
peppermint syrup vigorously over ice cubes until well
frosted. Half-fill a tall chilled highball glass with the
cracked ice and strain the cocktail over it. Fill with ginger
ale and dress with the cucumber and lime.*

SANGRÍA SECA ◄

SERVES 6
2 cups tomato juice
1 cup orange juice
3 measures lime juice
½ measure Tabasco sauce
2 teaspoons Worcestershire sauce
1 jalapeño pepper, seeded and finely chopped
celery salt
white pepper (preferably freshly ground)
cracked ice

Pour the tomato juice, orange juice, lime juice, and Tabasco and Worcestershire sauces into a pitcher. Add the chopped jalapeño and season with the celery salt and white pepper. Stir well, cover, and chill in the refrigerator for at least one hour. To serve, half-fill chilled highball glasses with cracked ice and strain the cocktail over it.

Sangría Seca makes a perfect long, cold drink for a crowd of friends at a summer barbecue—but without the alcohol. It's great for drivers and for those who have to stand around while others get a little merry.

POM POM

In this thirst quencher, lemonade is transformed into an extravaganza that's pretty in pink, with a frothy topping to match its frivolous name.

SERVES 1
juice of ½ a lemon
1 egg white
1 dash grenadine
crushed ice
lemon-flavored soda pop
lemon slice

Shake the lemon juice, egg white, and grenadine together over ice cubes and strain into a highball glass half-filled with crushed ice. Fill with the lemon-flavored soda pop and dress with a slice of lemon on the rim of the glass.

COCOBERRY ◂

SERVES 1
⅔ cup raspberries, plus a few to dress
crushed ice
1 measure coconut cream
⅔ cup pineapple juice
pineapple wedge

Rub the raspberries through a metal strainer with the back of a spoon and transfer the puree to a blender. Add the crushed ice, coconut cream, and pineapple juice. Blend until smooth, then pour the mixture, without straining, into a chilled lowball glass or highball glass. Dress with the pineapple wedge and fresh raspberries.

MOCHA SLUSH

Definitely for people with a sweet tooth, this is a chocoholic's dream and is popular with adults as well as children.

SERVES 1
crushed ice
2 measures coffee syrup
1 measure chocolate syrup
4 measures milk
grated chocolate

In a small blender, mix together the crushed ice, coffee syrup, chocolate syrup, and milk until slushy. Pour into a chilled wine glass and sprinkle with grated chocolate.

SALTY PUPPY ▴

SERVES 1
granulated sugar
coarse salt
wedge of lime
cracked ice
½ measure lime juice
grapefruit juice

Mix equal quantities of the sugar and salt together on a saucer. Rub the rim of a chilled highball glass with a wedge of lime and dip it into the sugar-and-salt mixture to frost it. Fill the glass with cracked ice and add the lime juice. Fill with grapefruit juice.

MINI COLADA ▲

Children love the flavor of coconut and milk, so this junior cocktail should be very popular.

SERVES 2
6 measures cold milk
4 measures pineapple juice
3 measures coconut cream
pineapple cubes
pineapple leaves
a few cocktail cherries

Shake the first three ingredients together over ice cubes until well chilled. Pour into highball glasses with more ice cubes, finish with pieces of pineapple, a pineapple leaf, and a cherry on a toothpick, and drink through straws.

KNICKS VICTORY COOLER ▲

SERVES 1
cracked ice
2 measures apricot juice
raspberry juice
spiral of orange peel
a few raspberries

Half-fill a chilled highball glass with the cracked ice. Pour the apricot juice over the ice, fill with raspberry juice, and stir gently. Decorate with a spiral of orange peel and fresh raspberries.

PEACHY CREAM ◂

SERVES 1

2 measures peach juice, chilled

2 measures light cream

cracked ice

Shake the peach juice and cream together over ice cubes vigorously until well frosted. Half-fill a chilled highball glass or lowball glass with cracked ice and strain the cocktail over it.

CLAM DIGGER

SERVES 1

Tabasco sauce

Worcestershire sauce

4 measures tomato juice

4 measures clam juice

¼ teaspoon horseradish sauce

cracked ice

celery salt

black pepper, freshly ground

celery stalk

lime wedge

Put ice cubes and the next five ingredients into a cocktail shaker and shake vigorously. Fill a chilled highball glass with the cracked ice and strain in the cocktail. Season to taste and dress with the celery and lime.

The Clam Digger is a good cocktail for a Sunday brunch, when alcoholic drinks can be too soporific and you end up wasting the rest of the day, but you still want something to wake up the taste buds and set them tingling.

VIRGIN MARY ☆ ▯

Simply a nonalcoholic Bloody Mary (page 98).

SERVES 1
3 measures tomato juice
1 measure lemon juice
2 dashes Worcestershire sauce
1 dash Tabasco sauce
cracked ice
celery salt
black pepper
lemon wedge
celery stalk

Shake the tomato juice, lemon juice, Worcestershire sauce, and Tabasco vigorously over cracked ice and season with celery salt and black pepper. Strain into an iced old-fashioned or lowball glass and add the lemon and celery.

GINGER FIZZ ▯

This is a cool, refreshing cocktail for a hot day that is easiest made in a blender.

SERVES 1
ginger ale
8 fresh mint leaves
cracked ice
a few raspberries
mint sprig

Put the ginger ale and several mint leaves into a blender and mix them together. Strain into a chilled highball glass two-thirds filled with cracked ice. Dress with the raspberries and a sprig of fresh mint.

SUNRISE ▲ ▯

SERVES 1
cracked ice
2 measures orange juice
1 measure lemon juice
1 measure grenadine
sparkling mineral water

Put the cracked ice into a chilled highball glass and pour the orange juice, lemon juice, and grenadine over it. Stir together well and fill with sparkling mineral water.

PEACHY MELBA

SERVES 1
3 measures peach juice
1 measure lemon juice
1 measure lime juice
1 measure grenadine
peach slice

Shake the peach juice, lemon juice, lime juice, and grenadine over ice cubes until well frosted. Strain into a chilled lowball glass and dress with a slice of peach.

PROHIBITION PUNCH ▲

SERVES 25
3¾ cups apple juice
1½ cups lemon juice
½ cup sugar syrup
cracked ice
9½ cups ginger ale
orange slices

Pour the apple juice, lemon juice, and sugar syrup into a large jug. Add the cracked ice and ginger ale. Stir gently to mix. Serve in chilled highball or lowball glasses with slices of orange and straws.

ITALIAN SODA

Italian syrup is available from most Italian delis and grocery stores and comes in a wide variety of flavors, including a range of fruits and nuts, so you can substitute your favorite and vary the volume to taste.

SERVES 1
cracked ice
1½ measures Italian hazelnut syrup
sparkling water
lime slice

Fill a chilled highball glass with cracked ice. Pour the hazelnut syrup over the ice and fill with sparkling water. Stir gently and decorate with the slice of lime.

HEAVENLY DAYS ▲

SERVES 1
2 measures hazelnut syrup
2 measures lemon juice
1 teaspoon grenadine
cracked ice
sparkling water
lime slice
starfruit (carambola) slice

Shake the hazelnut syrup, lemon juice, and grenadine vigorously over ice cubes until well frosted. Half-fill a highball glass with the cracked ice and strain the cocktail over it. Fill with sparkling water. Stir gently and dress with the slices of fruit.

COOL COLLINS ▶

SERVES 1
6 fresh mint leaves
1 teaspoon superfine sugar
2 measures lemon juice
cracked ice
sparkling water
mint sprig
lemon slice

Put the mint leaves into a chilled highball glass and add the superfine sugar and lemon juice. Crush the leaves with a spoon until the sugar has dissolved. Fill the glass with cracked ice and fill with sparkling water. Stir gently and decorate with a sprig of fresh mint and a slice of lemon.

218

BANANA COFFEE BREAK ◄

SERVES 2
1¼ cups milk
4 tablespoon instant coffee powder
⅔ cup vanilla ice cream
2 bananas, sliced and frozen
brown sugar to taste
fresh banana slices

Pour the milk into a food processor, add the coffee powder, and process gently until combined. Add half the vanilla ice cream and process gently, then add the remaining ice cream and process until well combined. When the mixture is thoroughly blended, add the bananas, sugar to taste, and process until smooth. Pour the mixture into highball or hurricane glasses and serve dressed with a few slices of banana.

ST CLEMENTS

SERVES 1
cracked ice
2 measures fresh orange juice
2 measures bitter lemon
orange slice
lemon slice

Put the cracked ice into a chilled highball glass. Pour in the orange juice and bitter lemon. Stir gently and dress with a slice of orange and a slice of lemon.

Thanks to the coffee, the Banana Coffee Break is a very adult-tasting, smoothie-style cocktail. In warm weather, it makes an excellent mid-morning pick-me-up.

CALIFORNIA SMOOTHIE

The secret of a successful smoothie, whether alcoholic or nonalcoholic, is to blend the mixture at medium speed until it is just smooth.

SERVES 1
1 banana, peeled and thinly sliced
½ cup strawberries, hulled
⅓ cup pitted dates
4½ teaspoons clear honey
1 cup orange juice
4–6 ice cubes, crushed

Put the banana, strawberries, dates, and honey into a blender and process until smooth. Add the orange juice and crushed ice and blend again until smooth. Pour into a chilled highball glass.

MOCHA CREAM

SERVES 2

1 scant cup milk
¼ cup light cream
1 tablespoon brown sugar
2 tablespoons unsweetened cocoa powder
1 tablespoon coffee syrup
6 ice cubes
a little whipped cream
grated chocolate

Put the milk, cream, and sugar into a food processor and process until combined. Add the cocoa powder and coffee syrup and process well. Then add the ice cubes and process until smooth. Pour the mixture into chilled highball glasses, and top with the whipped cream and some grated chocolate.

Although the Mocha Cream recipe looks as though it will be very rich, filling, and bad for the waistline, the resulting drink is actually quite light and delicate.

RED APPLE SUNSET ▲

SERVES 1

2 measures apple juice
2 measures grapefruit juice
dash of grenadine

Shake the apple juice, grapefruit juice, and a dash of grenadine over ice cubes until well frosted. Strain into a chilled cocktail glass.

UNDER THE BOARDWALK ▸ 🔲 🔳

SERVES 1
crushed ice
2 measures lemon juice
½ teaspoon sugar syrup
½ peach, peeled, pitted and chopped
sparkling water
a few raspberries

*Mix the crushed ice in a blender with the lemon juice,
sugar syrup, and peach until slushy. Pour into a chilled
highball glass or lowball glass. Fill with sparkling water
and stir gently. Dress with the raspberries.*

COCONUT ISLANDER 🔳

SERVES 4
1 pineapple
4 measures pineapple juice
4 tablespoon creamed coconut
4 measures milk
2 tablespoons crushed pineapple
3 tablespoons coconut flakes
crushed ice
cherries

*Cut the top off the pineapple and remove the flesh. Set
most of it aside for a dessert, but save a little to add to the
cocktail. Mix all the ingredients except the cherries in a
blender with a little crushed ice for 30–40 seconds. When
smooth and frothy, pour into the pineapple shell, decorate
with the cherries, and drink with straws.*

COCOBELLE 🔳

If you have a steady hand, this drink can be served
with pretty swirls of color up the sides.

SERVES 1
3 measures cold milk
1 measure coconut cream
2 scoops vanilla ice cream
3–4 ice cubes
grenadine
toasted long-shredded coconut or fresh coconut flakes

*Mix the milk, coconut cream, ice cream, and ice cubes
in a blender until slushy. Chill a highball glass and gently
dribble a few splashes of grenadine down the insides.
Pour the slush in slowly, so the color doesn't all dissolve at
once, and sprinkle the coconut on top.*

NEW ENGLAND PARTY ◄

SERVES 2
crushed ice
dash of Tabasco sauce
dash of Worcestershire sauce
1 teaspoon lemon juice
1 medium carrot, chopped
3 celery stalks, 2 chopped and 1 reserved
   whole to dress
1¼ cups tomato juice
⅔ cup clam juice
salt
black pepper, freshly ground

Put all the ingredients except the reserved celery into a blender and blend until smooth. Transfer to a pitcher, cover, and chill for about an hour. Pour into two chilled highball glasses and season. Dress with the celery stalk.

SLUSH PUPPY

Pink, pretty and refreshing—it looks serious, but you won't need to book a taxi to take you home.

SERVES 1
juice of 1 lemon or ½ pink grapefruit
½ measure grenadine
a few strips of lemon peel
2–3 teaspoons raspberry syrup
club soda
1 maraschino cherry

Fill a highball glass with ice cubes and pour in the lemon juice and grenadine. Add the lemon peel, syrup, and club soda to taste, and finish off with the cherry.

NONALCOHOLIC PIMM'S

SERVES 6
2 ½ cups lemon-flavored soda pop, chilled
2 scant cups cola, chilled
2 scant cups dry ginger ale, chilled
juice of 1 orange
juice of 1 lemon
a few drops of Angostura bitters
fruit slices
mint sprigs

Mix the lemon-flavored soda pop, cola, dry ginger, orange juice, lemon juice, and bitters together in a large pitcher or punch bowl. Float in the fruit slices and mint, store in a cold place, and add ice cubes at the last minute. Serve in chilled highball glasses for a really cooling effect.

The joy of Nonalcoholic Pimm's is that for occasions when you are drinking the real thing, drivers and the younger members of the family can also join in with no side effects.

THAI FRUIT COCKTAIL

When choosing your favorite combination of juices, make sure you use some of the more delicate oriental flavors.

SERVES 1
1 measure pineapple juice
1 measure orange juice
½ measure lime juice
1 measure passion fruit juice
2 measures guava juice
crushed ice
1 edible flower

Shake all of the juices together with the crushed ice. Pour into a chilled highball glass and decorate with a flower.

FRUIT COOLER ▲

This is a great breakfast energizer and gives you a healthy start to the day, once you've had your workout.

SERVES 2
1 cup orange juice
½ cup plain yogurt
2 eggs
2 bananas, sliced and frozen
fresh banana slices

Pour the orange juice and yogurt into a food processor and process gently until combined. Add the eggs and frozen bananas and process until smooth. Pour the mixture into highball or hurricane glasses and decorate the rims with slices of fresh banana.

APPLE FRAZZLE

SERVES 1

4 measures apple juice

1 teaspoon sugar syrup

½ teaspoon lemon juice

sparkling mineral water

Shake the apple juice, sugar syrup and lemon juice
vigorously over ice cubes until well frosted. Strain
into a chilled highball glass and fill with sparkling
mineral water.

SOBER SUNDAY

An interesting variation for those who aren't drinking
and anyone who is driving.

SERVES 1

cracked ice

1 measure grenadine

1 measure fresh lemon or lime juice

lemon-flavored soda pop

lemon slices

lime slices

Pour the grenadine and fruit juice into a highball glass
filled with cracked ice. Fill with the lemon-flavored soda
pop and finish with the lemon and lime slices.

FAUX KIR ROYALE ▲

SERVES 1

4–6 ice cubes, cracked

1½ measures raspberry syrup

sparkling apple juice, chilled

Put the cracked ice into a mixing glass and pour the
raspberry syrup over it. Stir well to mix, then strain into
a wine glass. Fill with chilled sparkling apple juice and stir.

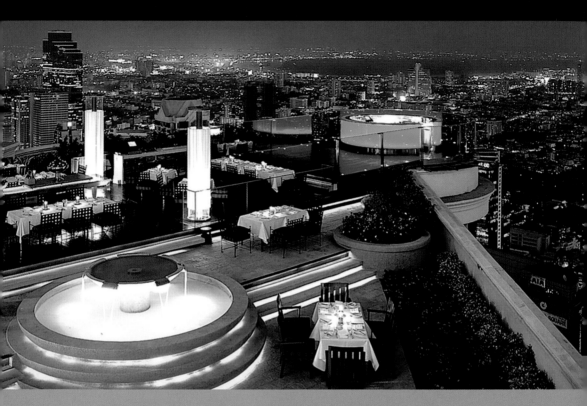

SKY BAR AT SIROCCO

BANGKOK

Sixty-three floors and 823 feet (247 m) up, yet still out in the open, the Sky Bar at Sirocco has been known to make the most blasé of travel writers gasp. Literally the world's most breathtaking watering hole, it has those who thought themselves totally impervious to vertigo at least thinking about it. Even without the hip crowd of local glitterati, no other bar has quite the same wow factor as this.

To arrive in this dramatic location, you take the elevator to the 64th floor "dome" of the State Tower, where an open-sided staircase descends one floor to an uncovered deck (closed in inclement weather). On one side is a restaurant. On the other the oval-shaped Sky Bar is cantilevered over the edge of the building, seeming to

BEST FOR

wow factor

SKY BAR COSMOPOLITAN

SERVES 1

2 tablespoons vodka

3 teaspoons Grand Marnier

1½ teaspoons crème de cassis

1½ teaspoons lime juice

2 tablespoons cranberry juice

orange peel

Shake the vodka, Grand Marnier, crème de cassis, lime juice, and cranberry juice vigorously in a shaker with ice cubes for ten seconds. Strain into a frosted Martini glass and garnish with the orange peel.

❖

"Sirocco's Sky Bar is one of the world's highest alfresco bars, so as you can imagine it has simply the most overwhelming views of Bangkok."

Senior restaurant manager,
Siriluk Pukalanont

defy gravity. A chest-high Plexiglass barrier is all that separates imbibers from the precipice.

Peering down from Bangkok's second-tallest skyscraper, the cars below look like ants and the Chao Phraya River a trickle. Previous guests have commented that the airplanes overhead seem just as close as the ground below. To add to the atmosphere, a jazz band plays and the illuminated bar is multihued, glowing blue, pink, and green, and changing color every few minutes.

Given everything else that's happening, what's most surprising is that the cocktails here are no afterthought. If you can take your eyes off the view, you'll notice there's an extensive cocktail menu using top-quality spirits. Sky Bar's cocktails are renowned for their strength, but for those who prefer to stay 100 percent sober in this heady environment, nonalcoholic drinks are also on the list.

SKY BAR AT SIROCCO

The Dome at State Tower

1055 Silom Rd.

Bangrak

Bangkok 10500

+66 2 624 9555

www.thedomebkk.com

Open daily

6:00 p.m. through 1:00 a.m.

AFTER DINNER

A good cocktail can be the perfect way to finish off a meal. You may forego dessert and opt for a fruity, creamy cocktail or you may choose something more astringent to aid digestion and set you up for another drink. Either way, one of these specially selected recipes is bound to suit.

POUSSE-CAFÉ ◂

A pousse-café is a layered cocktail of many different colored liqueurs. Each liqueur has a different density, so that when it's floated on top of the previous one it maintains its relative position in the glass.

SERVES 1
¼ measure grenadine
¼ measure crème de menthe
¼ measure Galliano
¼ measure kümmel
¼ measure brandy

Chill the grenadine, crème de menthe, Galliano, kümmel, and brandy.

Pour the grenadine into a chilled shot or pousse-café glass. Then carefully trickle the crème de menthe over the back of a spoon evenly over the grenadine. Repeat with the Galliano, kümmel, and brandy—in that order.

Well, enough of the theory. In practice it takes a certain amount of experience to gently but steadily pour the liqueurs over the back of a spoon. However, it's a skill that can be mastered.

Here are a couple of useful tips for making a Pousse-café. First, it is crucial to thoroughly chill all the liqueurs first and, second, always add the liqueurs in the order listed in the recipe. If you don't do these things, the cocktail will still taste delicious, but you can end up with an unsightly mess, which is definitely not the point of a Pousse-café.

SAVOY SANGAREE ▸   ☐ ♈

Port is a well known after-dinner drink. Here it is incorporated into a sophisticated cocktail.

SERVES 1
6 ice cubes, cracked
1 measure port
1 teaspoon superfine sugar
freshly grated nutmeg

Put the cracked ice into a mixing glass, pour in the port and superfine sugar, and stir until dissolved. Strain into a chilled cocktail glass or lowball glass and sprinkle with freshly grated nutmeg.

VODKA ESPRESSO   ♈

This makes a fabulous after-dinner treat. It's usually made with Stolichnaya vodka and Amarula, a South African cream liqueur with a caramel flavor.

SERVES 1
cracked ice
2 measures espresso or other strong brewed
   coffee, cooled
1 measure vodka
2 teaspoons superfine sugar
1 measure Amarula

Put the cracked ice into a cocktail shaker, pour in the coffee, vodka, and sugar. Cover, and shake vigorously for 10–20 seconds, until the outside of the shaker is misted. Strain into a cocktail glass, then float the Amarula on top.

STARS AND STRIPES ▸   ☐ ♈

SERVES 1
¾ measure cherry brandy, chilled
1½ measures light cream, chilled
¾ measure blue curaçao, chilled

Pour the chilled cherry brandy into a chilled shot glass or pousse-café glass. With a steady hand, gently pour in the chilled light cream using the back of a teaspoon to make a second layer and, finally, gently pour in the blue curaçao in the same way.

FANCY FREE

The key to this layered drink is to chill the liqueur and the glass in the freezer. If it does seem to mix on impact, give it a little time to settle and form its layers again.

SERVES 1
⅓ measure cherry brandy, iced
⅓ measure Cointreau, iced
⅓ measure apricot liqueur, iced

Into a chilled pousse-café or wine glass pour the cherry brandy. Then trickle in the Cointreau over the back of a spoon and repeat with the apricot liqueur.

GODDAUGHTER ▲

SERVES 1
4–6 ice cubes, crushed
2 measures applejack
1 measure amaretto
1 tablespoon applesauce
ground cinnamon

Put the crushed ice into a blender and add the applejack, amaretto, and applesauce. Blend until smooth, then pour the mixture, without straining, into a chilled wine glass. Sprinkle with the ground cinnamon and serve.

GODSON ▾

SERVES 1
4–6 ice cubes, cracked
2 measures amaretto
orange juice
orange slice

Put the cracked ice into a chilled highball glass. Pour in the amaretto and fill with the orange juice. Stir well to mix and decorate with the slice of orange.

GOLDEN CADILLAC ▲

SERVES 1
1 measure triple sec
1 measure Galliano
1 measure light cream

Shake the triple sec, Galliano, and light cream vigorously over ice cubes until well frosted. Strain the mixture into a chilled cocktail glass.

OLD PAL ▶

SERVES 1
2 measures rye whiskey
1½ measures Campari
1 measure sweet vermouth

Pour the rye whiskey, Campari, and sweet vermouth over ice cubes in a shaker and shake vigorously until well frosted. Strain into a chilled cocktail glass.

MQS ▶

SERVES 1
lemon wedge
superfine sugar
4–6 ice cubes, cracked
2 measures Scotch whisky
1 measure Drambuie
1 measure green Chartreuse

Rub the rim of a chilled cocktail glass with the wedge of lemon, then dip the glass into the superfine sugar to frost it. Put the cracked ice into a mixing glass and pour in the Scotch whisky, Drambuie, and green Chartreuse. Stir to mix and strain into the prepared glass.

Why the name Mary is so closely associated with cocktails is a mystery. Bloody Mary was, of course Mary Tudor (1516–58), while MQS is named after Mary Queen of Scots (1542–67). Be careful to strain this pleasingly strong mixture well, because it will be spoiled if watered down.

TRICOLOR ◀

SERVES 1

1 measure crème de menthe, chilled
1 measure Baileys Irish Cream, chilled
1 measure red maraschino, chilled

Pour the chilled crème de menthe into a chilled shot glass. With a steady hand, gently pour in the chilled Baileys Irish Cream over the back of a teaspoon to make a second layer and, for the final layer, repeat with the chilled red maraschino.

BLACK WIDOW

Not as wicked as its title suggests, but if you're feeling adventurous you could have it straight, on the rocks.

SERVES 1

⅔ measure dark rum
⅓ measure Southern Comfort
juice of ½ a lime
dash of curaçao
club soda
lime peel

Shake the dark rum, Southern Comfort, lime juice, and a dash of curaçao together well over ice cubes and strain into a chilled highball glass. Fill with club soda and finish with a twist of lime.

ELK'S OWN ▲

SERVES 1

2 measures rye whiskey
1 measure ruby port
½ measure lemon juice
1 teaspoon sugar syrup
1 egg white
starfruit (carambola) slices

Shake the rye whiskey, ruby port, lemon juice, sugar syrup, and egg white vigorously over ice cubes until well frosted. Strain into a chilled cocktail glass and dress with the starfruit (carambola) slices

BACCARAT ▸

Cocktails have always been enjoyed at casinos and go hand in hand with the atmosphere of risk and gamble.

SERVES 1
1 measure Jack Daniels
½ measure Dubonnet
2 dashes of crème de cassis

Shake the Jack Daniels, Dubonnet, and crème de cassis together well over ice cubes until frosted. Strain into a chilled cocktail glass.

GODMOTHER ▴

SERVES 1
4–6 ice cubes, cracked
2 measures vodka
1 measure amaretto

Put the cracked ice into a chilled lowball glass and pour the vodka and amaretto over it. Stir to mix.

Unsurprisingly, the recipe for the Godmother is a variant on the popular 1970s cocktail the Godfather, which also contains the Italian liqueur amaretto.

CHERRYCOLA ▲

SERVES 1
6–8 ice cubes, cracked
2 measures cherry brandy
1 measure lemon juice
cola
lemon slice

Half-fill a chilled highball glass or lowball glass with the cracked ice. Pour the cherry brandy and lemon juice over the ice. Top up with cola, stir gently, and decorate with the slice of lemon.

GODCHILD ▲

SERVES 1
4–6 ice cubes, crushed
1½ measures amaretto
1 measure vodka
1 measure light cream

Whizz the crushed ice in a blender with the amaretto, vodka, and light cream. Blend until smooth, then pour into a chilled champagne flute

B52

In this recipe, Kahlúa can easily be substituted for the dark crème de cacao.

SERVES 1
1 measure dark crème de cacao, chilled
1 measure Baileys Irish Cream, chilled
1 measure Grand Marnier, chilled

Pour the chilled dark crème de cacao into a shot glass or pousse-café glass. With a steady hand, gently pour in the chilled Baileys Irish Cream to make a second layer, then gently pour in the chilled Grand Marnier.

BEADLESTONE ▲

SERVES 1
4–6 ice cubes, cracked
2 measures Scotch whisky
1½ measures dry vermouth

Put the cracked ice into a mixing glass and pour over the Scotch whisky and dry vermouth. Stir well to mix and strain into a chilled cocktail glass.

INDIAN SUMMER

The coffee liqueur is the key ingredient in this delicious long mix—it would be good with crème de noyaux or crème de cacao too.

SERVES 1
1 measure vodka
2 measures Kahlúa
1 measure gin
2 measures pineapple juice
tonic water
lime slice
cucumber slice

Shake the vodka, Kahlúa, gin, and pineapple juice well over ice cubes until frosted. Strain into a cocktail glass or wine glass and fill with the tonic water. Dress with the lime and cucumber.

AVALANCHE ◄

This rich combination of almonds from the amaretto, and apricots from the brandy and juice is delicious after dinner, and you might want it instead of dessert.

SERVES 1
1 measure amaretto
½ measure apricot brandy
1 measure apricot or mango juice
1 scoop vanilla ice cream

Mix the Amaretto, apricot brandy, apricot or mango juice, and ice cream in a blender until well frosted and frothy. Pour into an iced cocktail glass and drink through a straw.

COWBOY

In movies, cowboys drink their rye straight, often pulling the cork out of the bottle with their teeth, and it is certainly difficult to imagine John Wayne or Clint Eastwood sipping delicately from a chilled cocktail glass, so use a lowball glass.

SERVES 1
3 measures rye whiskey
2 tablespoon light cream

Pour the whiskey and cream over ice cubes and shake vigorously until well frosted. Strain into a chilled lowball glass.

OSBORNE ▲

This cocktail was named for Queen Victoria's Isle of Wight residence and was, apparently, a favorite tipple of Her Majesty.

SERVES 1
3 measures claret
1 measure Scotch whisky

Pour the claret and Scotch whisky into a wine glass, stir, and serve.

JEALOUSY

If you want a change, you could occasionally flavor the cream in this excellent after-dinner cocktail with a different liqueur.

SERVES 1
1 teaspoon crème de menthe
1–2 tablespoons heavy cream
2 measures coffee or chocolate liqueur
chocolate matchsticks

Gently beat the crème de menthe into the cream until thick. Pour the coffee liqueur into a small iced cocktail glass and carefully spoon on the whipped, flavored cream. Serve with chocolate matchsticks.

WHISKEY SOUR

This drink originates in the Deep South and traditionally uses the best rye whiskey, but it can also be made with vodka, gin, or other spirits.

SERVES 1
1 measure lemon or lime juice
2 measures blended rye whiskey
1 teaspoon superfine sugar or syrup de gomme
lemon or lime slice
cocktail cherry

Shake the lemon or lime juice, blended whiskey, and superfine sugar well over ice cubes and strain into a sour glass. Finish with the slice of lemon or lime and the cherry.

MUDSLIDE

Despite its ominous-sounding name, this is a richly flavored creamy concoction that is beautiful whatever the weather.

SERVES 1
1½ measures Kahlúa
1½ measures Baileys Irish Cream
1½ measures vodka

Shake the Kahlúa, Baileys Irish Cream, and vodka vigorously over ice cubes until well frosted. Strain into a chilled wine glass.

BLACK BUSH

Bourbon whiskey has its own distinctive flavor, which is warm, rich, oakey, and brought out well here by the sloe gin.

SERVES 1
½ measure bourbon whiskey
½ measure sloe gin
4–6 ice cubes, cracked
fresh cherry

Stir the bourbon and sloe gin together with the cracked ice. Strain into a chilled cocktail glass and dress with the fresh cherry.

AMARETTO STINGER ‹

SERVES 1

2 measures amaretto

1 measure white crème de menthe

Pour the amaretto and white crème de menthe over ice cubes. Shake vigorously until well frosted and strain into a chilled cocktail glass or lowball glass.

GENOESE ‹

SERVES 1

1 measure vodka

1 measure grappa

½ measure Sambuca

½ measure dry vermouth

Vigorously shake the vodka, grappa, Sambuca, and dry vermouth over ice cubes until well frosted. Strain into a chilled cocktail glass.

RASPBERRY LIFTOFF ▸ ☆ ♟

If you're in need of a boost after a heavy meal, the fruity flavors and fizz of this cocktail will provide it, but for maximum lift make it with fresh juice and fruit, and the champagne should be freshly popped and bubbly.

SERVES 1
1 measure raspberry vodka
1 measure fresh raspberry juice
1 measure orange juice
champagne, chilled
raspberries

Shake the vodka, raspberry juice, and orange juice vigorously over ice cubes until well frosted. Strain into a chilled flute and fill with chilled champagne. Stir gently to mix and dress with the raspberries.

WHISKEY SANGAREE ▲ ▢

SERVES 1
6 ice cubes, cracked
2 measures bourbon
1 teaspoon sugar syrup
club soda
1 tablespoon ruby port
freshly grated nutmeg

Put the cracked ice into a chilled lowball glass. Pour on the bourbon and sugar syrup, and fill with club soda. Stir gently to mix, then float the ruby port on top. Sprinkle with the freshly grated nutmeg.

ASHLEY WILKES ◄

Ashely Wilkes, of course, is the object of Scarlett O'Hara's obsession in *Gone With The Wind* and this recipe certainly has the feel of the Old South.

SERVES 1
4 sprigs of fresh mint
1 teaspoon sugar
dash of lime juice
6 ice cubes, cracked
2 measures bourbon
1 measure peach brandy
sprig of mint

Crush three of the sprigs of mint and place them in a chilled highball glass. Add the sugar, lime juice, and cracked ice. Pour in the bourbon and peach brandy, and stir to mix. Dress with the remaining sprig of mint.

TOFFEE SPLIT

You're unlikely to need a dessert as well, but you could always pour this over some ice cream.

SERVES 1
crushed ice
2 measures Drambuie
1 measure toffee liqueur, iced

Fill a shot glass with crushed ice. Pour in the Drambuie and then pour on the toffee liqueur, carefully from the side of the glass, so it layers on top. Drink immediately.

KENTUCKY ORANGE BLOSSOM ►

SERVES 1
2 measures bourbon
1 measure orange juice
½ measure triple sec
orange wedge

Shake the bourbon, orange juice, and triple sec vigorously over ice cubes until well frosted. Strain into a chilled cocktail glass and dress with the wedge of orange.

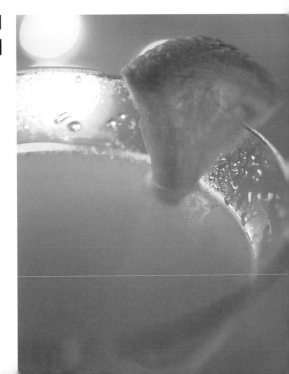

OLD ETONIAN ▲ 　 Ⓨ

SERVES 1
6–8 ice cubes, cracked
dash of crème de noyaux
dash of orange bitters
1 measure gin
1 measure Lillet
orange peel

*Put the cracked ice into a mixing glass and add the
dashes of crème de noyaux and orange bitters, then
the gin and Lillet. Stir well to mix, then strain into a chilled
cocktail glass. Squeeze a piece of orange peel into the
glass before serving.*

THISTLE ▲ 　 Ⓨ

SERVES 1
4–6 ice cubes, cracked
dash of Angostura bitters
2 measures Scotch whisky
1½ measures sweet vermouth

*Put the cracked ice into a mixing glass. Splash Angostura
bitters over the ice, then pour in the Scotch whisky and
sweet vermouth. Stir well to mix and strain into a chilled
cocktail glass.*

GREAT DANE ▾

SERVES 1

2 measures gin

1 measure cherry brandy

½ measure dry vermouth

1 teaspoon kirsch

twists of lemon peel

Shake the gin, cherry brandy, dry vermouth, and kirsch vigorously over ice cubes until well frosted. Strain into a chilled cocktail glass or highball glass and dress with the twists of lemon peel.

BLACK RUSSIAN

History records only White and Red Russians. The omission of the Black Russian is a sad oversight. For the coffee liqueur, you can use either Tia Maria or Kahlúa, depending on your personal taste. The latter is sweeter.

SERVES 1

4–6 ice cubes, cracked

2 measures vodka

1 measure coffee liqueur

Pour the vodka and liqueur over the cracked ice in a chilled lowball glass. Stir to mix.

To create a White Russian, follow the Black Russian recipe, then float a tablespoon of heavy cream on top. If you blend the ingredients instead, it becomes a Russian Coffee. For a Red Russian, substitute cherry brandy for the coffee liqueur, but don't add cream.

253

LONG GONE ▸

SERVES 1

2 measures bourbon
1 measure Drambuie
1 measure orange juice
dash of orange bitters
orange wedge

Shake the bourbon, Drambuie, orange juice, and dash of orange bitters vigorously over ice cubes, until well frosted. Strain into a chilled cocktail glass. Dress with the wedge of orange.

FIFTH AVENUE

After-dinner cocktails often include cream and this one also has the delicate flavors of apricot and cocoa.

SERVES 1

1 measure dark crème de cacao, iced
1 measure apricot brandy, iced
1 measure cream

Pour the crème de cacao into a chilled cocktail glass. Carefully add a layer of apricot brandy over the back of a spoon resting against the edge of the glass. Repeat with the cream. Each layer should float on top of the previous one.

CHOCOLATE STINGER ▸

A Stinger always contains crème de menthe. This version was concocted in the days of Prohibition, the sweet, minty liqueur being used to mask the flavor of the rotgut hard liquor available at the time.

SERVES 1

1 measure dark crème de cacao
1 measure white crème de menthe

Pour the dark crème de cacao and white crème de menthe over ice cubes. Shake vigorously until well frosted. Strain into a chilled cocktail glass or lowball glass.

LE BAR, HOTEL GEORGE V

PARIS

Opened in 1928 with a glitzy cocktail party to celebrate the launch of a transatlantic liner, the award-winning George V Hotel has an illustrious history. There are plenty of trendy see-and-be-seen drinking spots in the French capital today. However, this Le Bar (there are others similarly named) constantly wins plaudits for being a Belle Epoque oasis in a bustling contemporary city.

The bar staff also get a special mention for being not only impeccably professional, but also courteous and friendly, without the slightest whiff of Parisian *hauteur*. Both the high-society dames and wealthy financiers who come regularly for aperitifs, and those for whom a visit is a special event, are treated like royalty (remember to dress relatively elegantly).

BEST FOR
timeless elegance

TIME WAITS FOR NO ONE

While Le Bar is famous for its selection of Martinis, it has also recently created a menu using some of the world's oldest brandies, cognacs, whiskeys, and other spirits.

SERVES 1

cracked ice

½ cup dark rum

2 teaspoons honey

1 cinnamon stick

Fill a cocktail glass with cracked ice and let stand so that the ice chills the glass. Pour the dark rum and honey into a cocktail shaker and shake. Pour the mixture over the ice and stir with the cinnamon stick. Garnish with the cinnamon stick.

❖

"Le Bar has a very nice mix of Parisians and international guests from the hotel, not to mention some celebrities. This great crowd makes it typically Parisian— convivial and warm."

Head barman, Johann Burgos

The room itself is cosily lined with mahogany and what is aptly described as "cognac-colored" wood. As guests lounge in sumptuous leather sofas, they can also gaze through the large plate-glass window out onto Avenue George V beyond.

Some older customers fondly remember the barmen who issued "international mixing passports" and made the place even more legendary in the 1950s and 1960s. However, today's staff are upholding the standard with their Champagne Specials and stylishly presented fruit Martinis (sour apple and lychee are just two noteworthy flavors).

The hotel, which has accommodated so many world statesmen, was faithfully renovated by Four Seasons in the late 1990s, but its charming "olde worlde" bar has always been a classy reminder of the heyday of the cocktail era.

LE BAR

FOUR SEASONS HOTEL GEORGE V

31 Avenue George V

(near Rue Pierre Charron)

75008 Paris

+33 1 49 52 70 00

www.fourseasons.com/paris

Open

Sunday to Friday: 10:00 a.m. to 1:00 a.m.

Saturday: 10:00 a.m. to 2:00 a.m.

(3:00 p.m. to 6:00 p.m. cocktails

6:00 p.m. to 12:00 a.m. light entrées)

NIGHT OUT

Whether or not the point is to consume as much alcohol as possible, enjoying a cocktail or two with friends is an immensely pleasurable experience. If you intend to spend the evening in a bar, why not ask the bartender to mix one or more of these beauties for you?

TEQUILA SLAMMER ◂ ☆ ▯

Slammers are also known as shooters. The idea is that you pour the ingredients directly into the glass, without stirring. Cover the glass with one hand to prevent spillage, slam it on to a table to mix, and down the cocktail in one. Make sure you use a strong glass.

SERVES 1
1 measure white tequila, chilled
1 measure lemon juice
sparkling wine, chilled

Put the tequila and lemon juice into a chilled shot glass. Fill with sparkling wine. Cover the glass with your hand and slam on the table.

Unsurprisingly, this cocktail gets its name from the way it is commonly consumed. The slamming action releases bubbles of carbon dioxide, causing the drink to foam rather vigorously. It must be downed in one, otherwise the bubbles will escape.

If you try this at home, you can substitute lemon-flavored soda pop or ginger ale for the sparkling wine. You can also use real champagne, in which case the drink becomes a Slammer Royale.

Drinking slammers, or shooters, can mean that the drinker becomes intoxicated quickly. This is often exacerbated in a group situation where there can be a competitive element to drinking them.

ALABAMA SLAMMER

Small, but perfectly proportioned—this is a shooter with a real Southern kick.

SERVES 1
cracked ice
1 measure Southern Comfort
1 measure amaretto
1 measure sloe gin
½ teaspoon lemon juice

Pour the Southern Comfort, amaretto, and sloe gin over cracked ice in a mixing glass and stir. Strain into a shot glass and add the lemon juice. Cover with your hand and slam on the table.

ANKLE BREAKER ▲

SERVES 1
2 measures dark rum
1 measure cherry brandy
1 measure lime juice
1 teaspoon sugar syrup

Shake the dark rum, cherry brandy, lime juice, and sugar syrup over ice cubes until well frosted. Strain into a chilled highball or lowball glass.

STAR WARS ▶

"A long time ago in a galaxy far, far away…" this cocktail was invented—or maybe not.

SERVES 1
2 measures gin
2 measures lemon juice
1 measure Galliano
1 measure crème de noyaux
twist of lemon peel

Shake the gin, lemon juice, Galliano, and crème de noyaux vigorously over ice cubes until well frosted. Strain into a chilled cocktail glass and serve with the twist of lemon peel.

HUATUSCO WHAMMER ‹

SERVES 1
1 measure white tequila
½ measure white rum
½ measure vodka
½ measure gin
½ measure triple sec
1 measure lemon juice
½ teaspoon sugar syrup
cracked ice
cola

Shake the tequila, rum, vodka, gin, triple sec, lemon juice, and sugar syrup vigorously over ice cubes until well frosted. Fill a chilled highball glass with cracked ice and strain the cocktail over it. Fill with cola, stir gently, and serve with straws.

JOHN WOOD ﹀

SERVES 1
cracked ice
2 measures sweet vermouth
½ measure Irish whiskey
1 measure lemon juice
dash of Angostura bitters

Shake the vermouth, whiskey, and lemon juice vigorously over the cracked ice with a dash of Angostura bitters until well frosted. Strain into a chilled wine glass.

Vermouth is an immensely useful cocktail flavoring that contains more than 50 herbs and spices, and combines well with many spirits. It had fallen in popularity as a base for cocktails, but is now enjoying a revival.

CHESHIRE CAT ▸

This delicious concoction is sure to leave you grinning like the famous fictional feline character.

SERVES 1
cracked ice
1 measure brandy
1 measure sweet vermouth
1 measure orange juice
champagne, chilled
orange peel

Pour the brandy, sweet vermouth, and orange juice over cracked ice in a mixing glass. Stir well, then strain into a chilled flute and fill with the chilled champagne. Squeeze in a twist of orange peel and decorate with an orange peel spiral.

CHERRY KITSCH

This is a velvety smooth cocktail, fruity but with a rich brandy undertone. A touch of maraschino liqueur added at the end would be good too.

SERVES 1
crushed ice
1 measure cherry brandy
2 measures pineapple juice
½ measure kirsch
1 egg white
frozen maraschino cherry

Shake the cherry brandy, pineapple juice, kirsch, and egg white well over the crushed ice until frosted. Pour into a chilled highball glass and decorate with the frozen maraschino cherry.

MAGNOLIA BLOSSOM ▸

SERVES 1
2 measures gin
1 measure lemon juice
1 measure light cream

Shake the gin, lemon juice, and light cream vigorously over ice cubes until well frosted. Strain into a chilled cocktail glass.

CONEY ISLAND BABY ▸

SERVES 1
2 measures peppermint schnapps
1 measure dark crème de cacao
cracked ice
club soda

Shake the peppermint schnapps and dark crème de cacao vigorously over ice cubes until well frosted. Fill a chilled lowball glass with cracked ice and strain the cocktail over it. Fill with the club soda.

UNION JACK ◂

SERVES 1
1 measure maraschino, chilled
1 measure blue curaçao, chilled
1 measure grenadine, chilled

Pour the chilled maraschino into a chilled shot glass. With a steady hand, gently pour in the chilled blue curaçao to make a second layer and, finally, gently pour in the chilled grenadine.

VOODOO

This enthralling mixture of flavors is guaranteed to weave a spell on your taste buds and work its magic from the very first sip.

SERVES 1
½ measure Kahlúa, chilled
½ measure Malibu, chilled
½ measure butterscotch schnapps, chilled
1 measure milk, chilled

Pour the Kahlúa, Malibu, schnapps, and milk into a highball glass and stir well.

FLYING SCOTSMAN ▲

SERVES 1

4–6 ice cubes, crushed

dash of Angostura bitters

2 measures Scotch whisky

1 measure sweet vermouth

¼ teaspoon sugar syrup

*Put the crushed ice into a blender, splash the Angostura
bitters over the it, and add the Scotch whisky, sweet
vermouth, and sugar syrup. Blend until slushy and pour
into a chilled lowball glass.*

BANANA SLIP ▲

SERVES 1

1 measure crème de banane, chilled

1 measure Baileys Irish Cream, chilled

*Pour the chilled crème de banane into a shot glass. With
a steady hand, gently pour in the chilled Baileys Irish
Cream to make a second layer.*

AURORA BOREALIS ◀

SERVES 1

1 measure grappa or vodka, chilled
1 measure green Chartreuse, chilled
½ measure orange curaçao, chilled
few drops of crème de cassis, chilled

Pour the grappa slowly around one side of a well-chilled shot glass. Gently pour the Chartreuse around the other side. Pour the curaçao gently into the center and add a few drops of crème de cassis just before serving. Don't stir. Drink slowly.

FRENCH KISS

SERVES 1

2 measures bourbon
1 measure apricot liqueur
2 teaspoons grenadine
1 teaspoon lemon juice

Shake the bourbon, apricot liqueur, grenadine, and lemon juice vigorously over ice cubes until well frosted. Strain into a chilled cocktail glass.

The spectacular Aurora Borealis should not be mixed or stirred. Let it swirl around the glass, creating a multihued effect, and try to guess what the various flavors are.

FIREMAN'S SOUR ▸

SERVES 1

2 measures white rum

1½ measures lime juice

1 tablespoon grenadine

1 teaspoon syrup de gomme

cocktail cherry

Shake the white rum, lime juice, grenadine, and syrup de gomme over ice cubes until well frosted. Strain into a cocktail glass and decorate with the cocktail cherry.

BROADWAY SMILE ▴

SERVES 1

1 measure triple sec, chilled

1 measure crème de cassis, chilled

1 measure Swedish Punsch, chilled

Pour the triple sec into a chilled lowball glass. With a steady hand, pour the chilled crème de cassis on top, without mixing, and then pour the chilled Swedish Punsch on top, again without mixing.

FLYING GRASSHOPPER

There are two versions of this cocktail—one made with equal quantities of white and green crème de menthe and one with green crème de menthe and chocolate liqueur.

SERVES 1

cracked ice

1 measure vodka

1 measure green crème de menthe

1 measure white crème de menthe

Put the cracked ice into a mixing glass or pitcher and pour in the vodka and both types of crème de menthe. Stir well and strain into a highball glass.

PLANTATION PUNCH ◄ ☆ ▯

SERVES 1

2 measures dark rum

1 measure Southern Comfort

1 measure lemon juice

1 teaspoon brown sugar

sparkling water

1 teaspoon ruby port

lemon slice

orange slice

Shake the dark rum, Southern Comfort, and lemon juice vigorously over ice cubes with the brown sugar until well frosted. Strain into a chilled highball glass and fill, almost to the rim, with sparkling water. Float the ruby port on top by pouring it gently over the back of a teaspoon and garnish with the slices of lemon and orange.

CUBAN ◄ 🍸

SERVES 1

2 measures brandy

1 measure apricot brandy

1 measure lime juice

1 teaspoon white rum

Pour the brandy, apricot brandy, lime juice, and white rum over ice cubes and shake vigorously until well frosted. Strain into a chilled cocktail glass.

ARCHIPELAGO 🍸

In this cocktail a colorful selection of flavors and fruit from many places is topped with a layer of cream, almost like fruit salad and cream in a bowl.

SERVES 1

1¼ measures cognac

¾ measure kiwi juice or syrup

¼ measure mandarin liqueur

¼ measure chocolate liqueur

1 tablespoon light cream

kiwi slice or mint leaf

Stir the cognac, kiwi juice, mandarin liqueur, and chocolate liqueur together over ice cubes in a chilled mixing glass and strain into a cocktail glass. Carefully pour the cream in a layer over the top. Decorate with the kiwi slice or mint leaf.

MRS. FITZHERBERT ▼

This cocktail is named for Mrs. Fitzherbert, who secretly married the Prince of Wales, later George IV. Since she was a widow, a Catholic, and George III hadn't blessed the union, the prince was forced to divorce her and marry a wealthy Protestant princess instead. Rumor has it that when he died he wore a miniature of Mrs. Fitzherbert around his neck.

SERVES 1

1 measure white port
1 measure cherry brandy

Pour the white port and cherry brandy over ice cubes in a mixing glass. Stir to mix. Strain into a chilled cocktail glass.

BUTTAFUOCO ▶

SERVES 1

2 measures white tequila
½ measure Galliano
½ measure cherry brandy
½ measure lemon juice
cracked ice
club soda
cocktail cherry

Shake the white tequila, Galliano, cherry brandy, and lemon juice vigorously over ice cubes until well frosted. Half-fill a highball glass with cracked ice and strain the cocktail over it. Fill with the club soda and dress with the cocktail cherry.

AFRICAN MINT

Amarula is a very rich and exotic liqueur, which is best served and drunk really cold—but not on ice because that will dilute its real character.

SERVES 1

¾ measure crème de menthe, chilled
¾ measure Amarula, chilled

Pour the crème de menthe into the bottom of a shot glass, saving a few drops. Pour the Amarula slowly over the back of a spoon to create a layer over the minty liquid. Drizzle any remaining drops of mint over the creamy liqueur to finish.

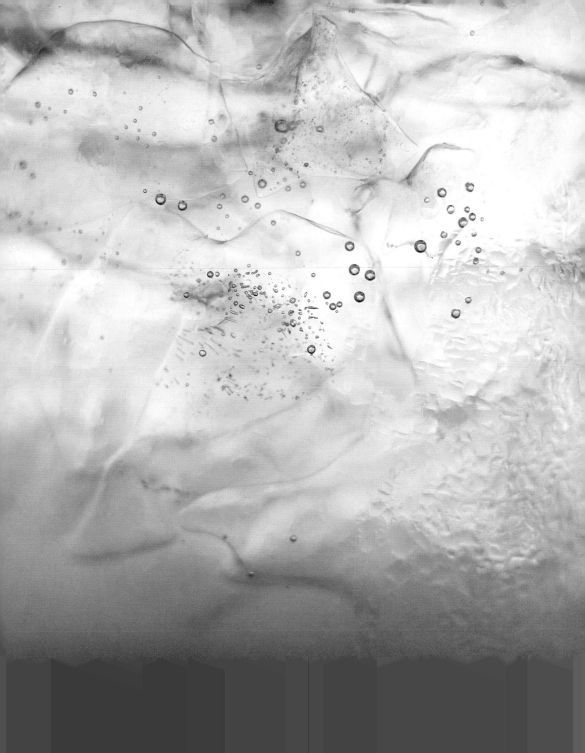

TEQUILA SHOT

SERVES 1
1 measure gold tequila
pinch of salt
lime wedge

Put one measure of gold tequila in a shot glass. Put the salt at the base of your thumb, between thumb and index finger. Hold the lime wedge in the same hand. Hold the shot of gold tequila in the other hand. Lick the salt, down the tequila, and suck the lime.

According to custom, the Tequila Shot is the only way to drink straight tequila. It is often described as being smooth and tart, so adding lime juice and salt may sound contradictory, but it works.

GREEN LADY ▲

SERVES 1
2 measures gin
1 measure green Chartreuse
dash of lime juice

Shake the gin, green Chartreuse, and dash of lime juice vigorously over ice cubes until well frosted. Strain into a chilled cocktail glass.

While less popular than peach or cherry eau de vie, pear brandy has a delicate fragrance and great flavor, but don't confuse it with pear liqueur.

SUPERIOR ROLLS-ROYCE ▲

SERVES 1
2 measures brandy
2 measures orange juice
1 measure triple sec

Shake the brandy, orange juice, and triple sec over ice cubes until well frosted. Strain into a chilled lowball glass.

PEARTINI

SERVES 1
1 teaspoon superfine sugar
pinch of ground cinnamon
lemon wedge
cracked ice
1 measure vodka
1 measure pear brandy, such as Poire William
   or Pera Segnana

Mix the sugar and cinnamon together on a saucer. Rub the outside rim of a cocktail glass with the lemon wedge, then dip the glass into the sugar-and-cinnamon mixture. Set aside. Put the cracked ice into a mixing glass or pitcher and pour in the vodka and pear brandy. Strain into the cocktail glass and serve.

GUMDROP MARTINI ◄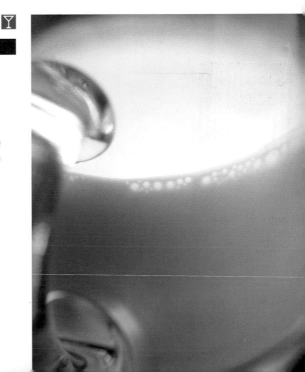

SERVES 1
lemon wedge
superfine sugar
2 measures lemon rum
1 measure vodka
½ measure Southern Comfort
½ measure lemon juice
½ teaspoon dry vermouth
gumdrops or other similar candies

Rub the rim of a chilled cocktail glass with the wedge of lemon, then dip the glass in a saucer of superfine sugar. Vigorously shake the lemon rum, vodka, Southern Comfort, lemon juice, and dry vermouth over ice cubes until well frosted. Strain into the prepared glass. Dress with the candies.

NUCLEAR FALLOUT

This is similar to a Pousse-Café (page 231), where the liqueurs are layered.

SERVES 1
1 teaspoon raspberry syrup
¼ measure maraschino
¼ measure yellow Chartreuse
¼ measure Cointreau
½ measure well-chilled blue curaçao

Chill all of the liqueurs, but especially the blue curaçao—put it in the coldest part of the freezer. Also chill a shot, or pousse-café glass. Carefully pour the raspberry syrup, then the maraschino, yellow Chartreuse, and Cointreau in layers over the back of a teaspoon. Finally, pour in the blue curaçao and wait for the fallout.

BLUE LADY

SERVES 1
2½ measures blue curaçao
1 measure white crème de cacao
1 measure light cream

Shake the blue curaçao, white crème de cacao, and light cream over ice cubes until well frosted. Strain into a chilled cocktail glass.

ZOMBIE ◄ ⭐ ▯

SERVES 1
crushed ice
2 measures dark rum
2 measures white rum
1 measure golden rum
1 measure triple sec
1 measure lime juice
1 measure orange juice
1 tablespoon grenadine
1 tablespoon orgeat syrup
1 teaspoon Pernod

Put crushed ice in a blender with the dark rum, white rum, golden rum, triple sec, fruit juices, grenadine, orgeat syrup, and Pernod. Blend until smooth. Pour, without straining, into a chilled highball glass.

ZIPPER ▯

This shooter gets its name from an unusual, not to say "weird" method of serving it, but it tastes just as good if served more conventionally.

SERVES 1
crushed ice
1 measure tequila
½ measure Grand Marnier
½ measure light cream

Vigorously shake the tequila, Grand Marnier, and cream over the crushed ice for 10–20 seconds, until the outside of the shaker is misted. Strain into a shot glass.

BARBED WIRE ► ▯ ▽

SERVES 1
3 measures vodka
1 teaspoon sweet vermouth
½ teaspoon Pernod
½ measure dry sherry
twist of lemon peel

Shake the vodka, sweet vermouth, Pernod, and dry sherry over ice cubes until well frosted. Strain into a chilled wine glass or cocktail glass and decorate with the twist of lemon peel.

ROYAL MATADOR ◄

SERVES 2
1 pineapple
8–10 ice cubes, crushed
4 measures golden tequila
1½ measures framboise
2 measures lime juice
1 tablespoon amaretto
starfruit (carambola) slice

Cut the top off the pineapple and reserve the lid. Scoop out the flesh, leaving the shell intact. Put the flesh in a blender and puree. Strain the juice from the puree and return it to the blender. Add the crushed ice, golden tequila, framboise, lime juice, and amaretto. Blend until slushy, then pour into the pineapple shell, adding more ice if required. Replace the lid and serve with straws and the slice of starfruit (carambola).

ORANGE PLANTER'S PUNCH

SERVES 1
1 measure rum
1 measure orange curaçao
2 dashes of Angostura bitters
1 teaspoon grenadine
juice of 1½ limes
cracked ice

Vigorously shake the rum, orange curaçao, Angostura bitters, grenadine, and lime juice over ice cubes until well frosted. Half-fill a chilled highball glass with cracked ice and strain the cocktail over it.

WHITE SPIDER ◄

If you've drunk your fill of cocktails and are thinking about heading home, this is a good one with which to finish the evening off.

SERVES 1
1 measure vodka
1 measure white crème de menthe

Pour the vodka and white crème de menthe over ice cubes in a mixing glass. Stir well and strain into a chilled cocktail glass.

AFTER FIVE

Originally the name of a mixed cocktail filled with lemon-flavored soda pop or club soda, the After Five has now been completely transformed into a layered shooter with a real kick.

SERVES 1
½ measure peppermint schnapps, chilled
1 measure Kahlúa, chilled
1 tablespoon Baileys Irish Cream, chilled

Pour the peppermint schnapps into a shot glass. Carefully pour the Kahlúa over the back of a teaspoon so that it forms a separate layer. Finally, float the Baileys Irish Cream on top.

SUBMARINO ▸

SERVES 1
1 cup Mexican beer
2 measures white tequila

Pour the Mexican beer into a chilled beer glass or tankard. Then pour the white tequila into a chilled shot glass and gently submerge the shot glass in the beer.

TEQUINI ▸

As the name suggests, this is a nice version of the Martini, that uses tequila instead of gin or vodka.

SERVES 1
cracked ice
3 measures white tequila
½ measure dry vermouth
dash of Angostura bitters
twist of lemon

Pour the white tequila and dry vermouth over cracked ice in a mixing glass. Add the dash of Angostura bitters and stir well. Strain into a chilled martini or cocktail glass and dress with a twist of lemon.

NELL GWYNNE ◄

Nell Gwynne was famously the mistress of seventeenth-century English king Charles II. When he first met her she was an orange seller in London's Covent Garden, so it is not surprising that a cocktail named after her is based on the orange-flavored liqueur triple sec.

SERVES 1

1 measure triple sec

1 measure peach schnapps

1 measure white crème de menthe

twist of lemon peel

Pour the triple sec, peach schnapps, and white crème de menthe over ice cubes in a mixing glass and stir well. Strain into a chilled cocktail glass and decorate with the twist of lemon peel.

NEGRONI

SERVES 1

1 measure gin

1 measure sweet vermouth

1 measure Campari

club soda

orange slice

Shake the gin, sweet vermouth, and Campari vigorously over ice cubes. Strain into a chilled cocktail glass, fill with the club soda if desired, and decorate with the slice of orange.

CHOCOLATE MARTINI ◄

SERVES 1

orange slice

cocoa powder

2 measures vodka

¼ measure crème de cacao

2 dashes orange flower water

twist of orange peel

Moisten the rim of a cocktail glass with the orange slice. Dip the rim in the cocoa powder and set aside. Shake the vodka, crème de cacao, and orange flower water over ice cubes until really well frosted. Strain into the cocktail glass and decorate with a twist of orange peel.

THE HAWKSMOOR

LONDON

Although it bears the name of an English baroque architect and evinces the scruffy-chic style of London's trendy Shoreditch district, this East End bar has built its world-class reputation on a classic American cocktail list. The beautiful cocktail menu is relatively brief, with around 50 choices, but it contains an entire section of bourbon-based Juleps, alongside a peppering of Algonquins, Brooklyns, Manhattans, Old-Fashioneds, and Sours.

Many of these drinks date back to pre-Prohibition days in the Deep South. While the Hawksmoor is against overly complicated drinks—its Kentucky Mint Julep, for example, uses mint infused in sugar syrup, bourbon, and nothing else—it does like to produce its

BEST FOR
classic American cocktails

LICORICE WHISKEY SOUR

This version of the traditional Whiskey Sour is a great example of how to evolve a classic effectively. To make the licorice syrup, put one cup of water and one cup of superfine sugar in a pan and bring to a boil. Then add three to four sticks of chopped licorice root and bring back to a boil. Cool and strain through cheesecloth.

SERVES 1

2 measures Buffalo
    Trace bourbon
2 tablespoons licorice syrup
dash of Angostura bitters
dash of egg white
grated licorice root

Shake the bourbon, licorice syrup, Angostura bitters, and egg white together over ice cubes. Strain the liquid twice, then pour into a small coupette glass. Garnish with the grated licorice root.

❖

"I think it's legitimate to say that the United States invented the cocktail, but cocktails evolve over time and you can choose where you want to dip into that history."

General manager, Nick Strangeway

own modern twists. General manager and celebrity mixologist Nick Strangeway is a firm believer in updating the classics for modern consumers. The Juleps, Algonquins (a pineapple-flavored favorite of writer and wit Dorothy Parker), and Sours, for example, are based on darker spirits such as rum, bourbon, and rye whiskey. The award-winning staff have had a little light-headed fun with a couple of gin fizzes too.

The place's playful sense of humor is also conveyed in its kitschy names, such as Tweeked Tikis and Leilani's Grass Hut, plus some world-beating punches, of which Strangeway is the grand master, all served up in an eclectic collection of vintage glassware that fits perfectly with the brick interior and long teak bar, salvaged from a 1930s' dance-hall. Nicholas Hawksmoor, who designed Christ Church Spitalfields just down the road, probably wouldn't know what to make of it.

THE HAWKSMOOR
157 Commercial Street
London E1 6BJ
+44 20 7247 7392
www.thehawksmoor.com

Open Monday through Saturday
Monday, Tuesday, and Wednesday
12:00 p.m. to 12:00 a.m.
Thursday and Friday
12:00 p.m. through 1:00 a.m.
Saturday
6:00 p.m. through 1:00 a.m.

PARTY INVITATION

If you're the host, you'll find recipes here that will impress when made in volume, as well as recipes that will stun when made on an individual basis. All are guaranteed to make your party go with that elusive swing. So if you're a guest, simply raise your cocktail glass and enjoy.

CAIPIRINHA ‹

This classic Brazilian cocktail is based on the sugarcane spirit cachaça. If you find it too sharp, add a little more sugar.

SERVES 1
6 lime wedges
2 teaspoons granulated sugar
3 measures cachaça
cracked ice
lime wedge

Put the lime wedges and sugar in a chilled lowball glass, and muddle them to release the lime juice. Pour on the cachaça, fill up the glass with the cracked ice, and stir well. Serve with the wedge of lime.

The name "Caipirinha" translates loosely as "country cousin" or "hayseed." However, the Caipirinha cocktail, often described as the national drink of Brazil, is now popular around the world, and is actually a sophisticated drink that delivers quite a kick.

The key to making a good Caipirinha is the way you muddle the limes and the sugar, to release the oils from the fruit peel.

Premium-quality cachaça is now available in most liquor stores, but if you can't find it, use vodka and make a Caipiroska instead. If you've got rum, make a Caipirissima. If you find either of these too strong, add a little more sugar. Another variant is the Caipifruta, which consists of cachaça, just about any crushed fresh fruit or fruits, condensed milk, and crushed ice.

MARGARITA GELATIN SHOT ▯

SERVES 10
3 lime wedges
2 tablespoons table salt
1 package lime gelatin
1¼ cups hot water
4–5 tablespoons Cointreau
1 cup tequila

Rub the outside rims of ten shot glasses with the lime wedges, then dip in the salt to frost them. Set aside. Break up the gelatin and place it in a heatproof measuring pitcher. Add the hot water and stir until the gelatin has dissolved. Let cool, then stir in the Cointreau and tequila to make the mixture up to 2½ cups. Divide the gelatin liquid among the prepared glasses, being careful to avoid disturbing the salt frosting, and chill in the refrigerator until set.

It is not essential to frost the glasses with salt for the Margarita Gelatin Shot, but it looks more attractive and pays homage to the original classic Margarita cocktail recipe of 1942.

TEQUILA COCKTAIL ▲ ☆ Ⓨ

SERVES 1
dash of Angostura bitters
3 measures golden tequila
1 measure lime juice
½ measure grenadine

Shake the dash of Angostura bitters, golden tequila, lime juice, and grenadine vigorously over ice cubes until well frosted, then strain into a chilled cocktail glass.

IRISH EYES ▸

SERVES 1
4–6 ice cubes, cracked
2 measures Irish whiskey
½ measure green Chartreuse

*Put the cracked ice into a mixing glass. Pour the Irish
whiskey and green Chartreuse over the ice. Stir well
and strain into a chilled cocktail or lowball glass.*

MILLIONAIRE COCKTAIL ▸

SERVES 1
⅔ measure bourbon
⅓ measure Cointreau
2 dashes of grenadine
1 egg white

*Shake the bourbon, Cointreau, grenadine, and egg
white over ice cubes and strain into a cocktail glass.*

EL DIABLO ▸

One or two Diablos and you'll certainly feel a bit of a
devil, but one or two too many and you'll feel like the
very devil.

SERVES 1
cracked ice
2–3 strips of lime peel
1 measure lime juice
3 measures white tequila
1 measure crème de cassis
twist of lime peel

*Fill a chilled lowball glass with the cracked ice, add the
lime peel, lime juice, tequila, and crème de cassis. Stir
well to mix. Serve with a twist of lime peel.*

CHRISTMAS PUNCH ▴

SERVES 8
1 quart red wine
4 tablespoons sugar
1 cinnamon stick
1½ cups boiling water
⅓ cup brandy
⅓ cup sherry
⅓ cup orange liqueur
2 seedless oranges, cut into wedges
2 apples, cored and cut into wedges

*Put the wine, sugar, and cinnamon into a large pan.
Warm over a low heat, stirring, until the mixture just starts
to simmer, but don't let it boil. Remove from the heat and
strain. Discard the cinnamon stick. Return the wine to the
pan and add the remaining ingredients. Warm gently over
a very low heat. Serve hot in heatproof glasses.*

In the bleak midwinter a glass
of this piping hot Christmas
Punch will warm the cockles
of anyone's heart. Remember,
do not let the mixture boil
because this will make much
of the alcohol evaporate.
Simmer gently.

SCREWDRIVER ☆ 🎴

This cocktail has universal appeal, and is great to serve to guests at a party if you're not sure of individual tastes. Freshly squeezed orange juice is a must.

SERVES 1
cracked ice
2 measures vodka
orange juice
orange slice

Fill a chilled highball glass with the cracked ice. Pour the vodka over the ice and fill with orange juice. Stir well to mix and dress with the slice of orange.

A number of cocktails are known simply by their initials. In this classic recipe BVD stands for brandy, vermouth, and Dubonnet. Strangely, although it retains the name, a modern BVD contains white rum, gin, and dry vermouth.

BVD ▲ ☆ 🍸

SERVES 1
cracked ice
1 measure brandy
1 measure dry vermouth
1 measure Dubonnet

Pour the brandy, dry vermouth, and Dubonnet over cracked ice in a mixing glass. Stir to mix and strain into a chilled cocktail glass.

DIAMOND HEAD ▾

SERVES 2
4 measures gin
2 measures lemon juice
1 measure apricot brandy
1 teaspoon sugar
1 egg white
spirals of lemon peel

Shake the gin, lemon juice, apricot brandy, sugar, and egg white vigorously over ice cubes until well frosted. Strain into two chilled cocktail glasses and serve with some spirals of lemon peel.

LEAP YEAR ▴

SERVES 1
2 measures gin
½ measure Grand Marnier
½ measure sweet vermouth
½ teaspoon lemon juice

Shake the gin, Grand Marnier, sweet vermouth, and lemon juice vigorously over ice cubes until well frosted. Strain into a chilled cocktail glass.

CHAMPAGNE SIDECAR ‹

SERVES 1
4–6 ice cubes, cracked
2 measures brandy
1 measure triple sec
1 measure lemon juice
champagne, chilled
twist of orange peel

Vigorously shake the brandy, triple sec, and lemon juice over the cracked ice until a frost forms. Strain into a chilled flute and fill it up with the chilled champagne. Dress with a twist of orange peel.

SANGRIA

A perfect long cold drink for a summer party.

SERVES 6
juice of 1 orange
juice of 1 lemon
2 tablespoons superfine sugar
1 orange, thinly sliced
1 lemon, thinly sliced
1 bottle red wine, chilled
lemon-flavored soda pop

Stir the orange juice, lemon juice, and sugar together in a large bowl or pitcher. When the sugar has dissolved, add a few ice cubes, the sliced orange and lemon, and wine. Marinate for one hour, then add the lemon-flavored soda pop and a few more ice cubes. Serve in wine glasses or highball glasses

Cointreau is the best-known brand of orange-flavored liqueur, but a Champagne Sidecar calls for triple sec, which is drier and stronger than curaçao and always colorless.

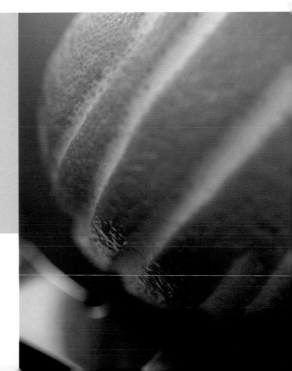

Make the stunning ice cubes required by the Louisa well in advance and remove them from the freezer at the very last second—they melt almost immediately.

LOUISA ▲

Blue cocktails are fun, so enhance the effect with a few colored ice cubes—make your ice cubes by adding a couple of drops of blue food coloring.

SERVES 1
6–8 ice cubes, cracked
¾ measure blue curaçao
½ measure vodka
¼ measure barley water
dash of lemon juice
club soda
blue ice cubes (see above)

Fill a highball glass with the cracked ice, add the blue curaçao, vodka, barley water, and lemon juice, and mix well. Fill with the club soda, but leave enough room for the blue ice cubes, which you should add just before serving.

MINTED DIAMONDS ▸

SERVES 1
1 teaspoon green crème de menthe
1 tablespoon ice water
1 measure white crème de menthe
2 measures apple or pear schnapps

Mix the green crème de menthe with the ice water, spoon the mixture into one or two compartments of an ice-cube tray, and freeze for about two hours. Stir the white crème de menthe and apple or pear schnapps over ice cubes until well frosted. Strain the liquid into a chilled cocktail glass and float the mint ice cubes on top at the last moment. Don't start drinking until the mint cubes begin to melt.

BRANDY COCKTAIL

SERVES 1
dash of Angostura bitters
2 measures brandy
½ teaspoon sugar syrup
lemon peel

Shake the dash of Angostura bitters, brandy, and sugar syrup vigorously over ice cubes until well frosted. Strain into a chilled cocktail glass and decorate with the twist of lemon peel.

MELANIE HAMILTON ◄

SERVES 1
2 measures triple sec
1 measure Midori
2 measures orange juice
cantaloupe melon wedge

Shake the triple sec, Midori, and orange juice vigorously over ice cubes until well frosted. Strain the mixture into a chilled cocktail glass and dress with the wedge of cantaloupe melon.

NAVAJO TRAIL ▲

SERVES 1
2 measures white tequila
1 measure triple sec
1 measure lime juice
1 measure cranberry juice

Pour the white tequila, triple sec, lime juice, and cranberry juice over ice cubes and shake vigorously until well frosted. Strain into a chilled cocktail glass.

WHISKEY SLING ▾

SERVES 1
1 teaspoon sugar
1 measure lemon juice
1 teaspoon water
2 measures blended rye whiskey
cracked ice
orange slice

In a mixing glass, stir the sugar, lemon juice, and water together until the sugar has dissolved. Pour in the rye whiskey and stir to mix. Half-fill a chilled lowball glass with the cracked ice and strain the cocktail over it. Decorate with the orange slice.

QUEEN OF MEMPHIS ▸

SERVES 1
2 measures bourbon
1 measure Midori
1 measure peach juice
dash of maraschino
melon wedge

Shake the bourbon, Midori, peach juice, and dash of maraschino vigorously over ice cubes until well frosted. Strain into a chilled cocktail glass and dress with the wedge of melon.

PEPPERMINT PATTY

Sometimes the simple things in life are the best—one such pleasure is this delicious combination of chocolate and peppermint.

SERVES 1
1 measure white crème de cacao
1 measure white crème de menthe

Vigorously shake the crème de cacao and crème de menthe over ice cubes for 10–20 seconds, or until the outside of the shaker is misted. Strain into a shot glass or cocktail glass.

PINK HEATHER ▶

SERVES 1

1 measure Scotch whisky
1 measure strawberry liqueur
sparkling wine, chilled
1 strawberry

Pour the Scotch whisky and strawberry liqueur into a chilled champagne flute. Fill with the chilled sparkling wine and dress with the strawberry.

SHILLELAGH ◀

A shillelagh (pronounced shee-lay-lee) is a wooden cudgel, traditionally made from blackthorn. Undoubtedly, this is a cocktail that hits the spot.

SERVES 1

2 measures Irish whiskey
1 measure dry sherry
1 teaspoon golden rum
1 teaspoon lemon juice
pinch of superfine sugar
cocktail cherry

Shake the Irish whiskey, dry sherry, golden rum, lemon juice and pinch of superfine sugar vigorously over ice cubes until well frosted. Strain into a chilled cocktail glass and dress with the cocktail cherry.

BRAIN HEMORRHAGE

This is a rare instance of a cocktail that is deliberately intended to look unpleasant, rather than tempting. It was probably invented to drink at Halloween.

SERVES 1

1 measure peach schnapps, chilled
1 teaspoon Baileys Irish Cream, chilled
½ teaspoon grenadine, chilled

Pour the peach schnapps into a shot glass, then carefully float the Baileys on top. Finally, top with the grenadine.

BULLDOG BREED ▸

SERVES 1
cracked ice
1 measure gin
2 measures orange juice
ginger ale, chilled

Half-fill a chilled highball glass or lowball glass with cracked ice. Pour the gin and orange juice over and fill with chilled ginger ale. Stir.

AROUND THE WORLD ▲

SERVES 1
1 measure Mandarine Napoleon
1 measure Polish vodka
½ measure Campari
½ measure crème de banane
½ measure coconut liqueur
cracked ice
lemon-flavored soda pop
kumquats, halved

Shake the Mandarine Napoleon, Polish vodka, Campari, crème de banane, and coconut liqueur over ice cubes until frosted. Fill a highball or lowball glass with the cracked ice, strain in the liquid, and fill with lemon-flavored soda pop. Decorate with the kumquat segments.

As you can see from the name, flavors from all "around the world" go into this glorious cocktail, so save it for a cosmopolitan occasion.

MARGARITA ☆ 🍸

A number of people claim to have invented the Margarita, but what is certain is that it is now one of the world's most popular cocktails.

SERVES 1
2 lime wedges
salt
3 measures white tequila
1 measure Cointreau or triple sec
2 measures lime juice

Rub the rim of a chilled cocktail glass with one of the wedges of lime and dip the glass into the salt to frost it. Vigorously shake the tequila, Cointreau, and lime juice over ice cubes until well frosted. Strain into the prepared glass, squeeze the remaining lime wedge over the top, and then drop it in.

The Margarita is a civilized version of the original way to drink tequila—with a lick of salt, a suck of lime juice, and a shot of tequila.

SELF-DESTRUCT ▾

SERVES 1
3 measures vodka
½ teaspoon lime juice
½ teaspoon triple sec

Shake the vodka, lime juice, and triple sec over ice cubes until well frosted. Strain into a chilled cocktail glass.

PINK PUSSYCAT ▴

Although it's not the only ingredient you can use to make a pink drink, a dash of grenadine will usually give your cocktail a reddish blush.

SERVES 1
cracked ice
dash of grenadine
2 measures gin
pineapple juice
pineapple slice

Half-fill a chilled highball glass with the cracked ice. Splash the grenadine over the ice and pour in the gin. Fill with the pineapple juice and dress with the slice of pineapple.

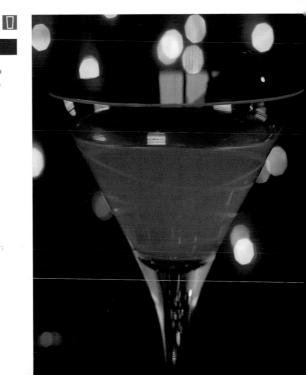

KISS KISS

SERVES 1
cracked ice
1 measure cherry brandy
1 measure gin
1 measure sweet vermouth

Half-fill a mixing glass with cracked ice and pour the cherry brandy, gin, and sweet vermouth over it. Stir well, then strain into a chilled cocktail glass.

ARTILLERY PUNCH ▸

SERVES 30
1 quart bourbon
1 quart red wine
1 quart strong, black tea
2 cups dark rum
1 cup gin
1 cup apricot brandy
4 measures lemon juice
4 measures lime juice
4 tablespoon sugar syrup
large block of ice
orange slices, thinly cut

Pour all the liquids and sugar syrup into a large bowl. Refrigerate for two hours. Place a large block of ice in a punch bowl. Pour the punch over the ice and decorate with the slices of orange. Serve in highball glasses.

TAILGATE ◂

SERVES 1
6 ice cubes, cracked
dash of orange bitters
2 measures vodka
1 measure green Chartreuse
1 measure sweet vermouth

Put the cracked ice into a mixing glass. Splash the orange bitters over the ice and pour in the vodka, green Chartreuse, and sweet vermouth. Stir well to mix, then strain into a chilled cocktail glass.

PINEAPPLE PLANTER'S PUNCH ◄ 🍸

SERVES 1

1 measure white rum
1 measure pineapple juice
juice of ½ a lime
½ measure curaçao
cracked ice
dash of maraschino
kiwi wedge
pineapple wedge

Mix the white rum, pineapple juice, lime juice, curaçao, and dash of maraschino together. Serve in a highball glass with the cracked ice and fruit wedges.

GIN SANGAREE ▲   🍸 🥃

SERVES 1

6–8 ice cubes, cracked
2 measures gin
½ teaspoon sugar syrup
sparkling water
1 tablespoon port
nutmeg, freshly grated

Put the cracked ice into a chilled highball glass or lowball glass. Pour the gin and sugar syrup over the ice and fill with the sparkling water. Stir gently to mix, then float the port on top. Sprinkle with the freshly grated nutmeg.

The word *Sangaree* is derived from the Spanish word for blood and Sangarees were once made with wine. Nowadays, they are more likely to have a spirit base, but whatever is used, the cocktail is invariably flavored with fresh nutmeg.

WILD WOMEN ▸

SERVES 1

2 measures bourbon

1 measure Pernod

1 measure apple juice

dash of Angostura bitters

apple slice

Shake the bourbon, Pernod, apple juice, and dash of Angostura bitters vigorously over ice cubes until well frosted. Strain into a chilled cocktail glass and dress with the slice of apple.

CREOLE LADY

SERVES 1

cracked ice

2 measures bourbon

1½ measures madeira

1 teaspoon grenadine

cocktail cherries

Pour the bourbon, madeira, and grenadine over cracked ice in a mixing glass. Stir well to mix, then strain into a chilled cocktail glass. Dress with the cocktail cherries.

PINK WHISKERS ▸

SERVES 1

2 measures apricot brandy

1 measure dry vermouth

2 measures orange juice

dash of grenadine

Shake the apricot brandy, dry vermouth, orange juice, and dash of grenadine vigorously over ice cubes until well frosted. Strain the mixture into a chilled cocktail glass.

SOUTHERN PEACH ◀ [Y] [□]

SERVES 1
cracked ice
1 measure Southern Comfort
1 measure peach brandy
1 measure light cream
dash of Angostura bitters
peach slice

Shake the Southern Comfort, peach brandy, and light cream with a dash of Angostura bitters vigorously over cracked ice until well frosted. Strain the mixture into a chilled cocktail glass or lowball glass and dress with the slice of peach.

TROPICAL FRUIT PUNCH ▾ [☆] [□]

SERVES 6
1 small ripe mango
4 tablespoons lime juice
1 teaspoon fresh ginger, finely grated
1 tablespoon light brown sugar
1¼ cups orange juice
1¼ cups pineapple juice
⅓ cup rum
crushed ice
orange slices
lime slices
pineapple slices
pineapple leaves
starfruit (carambola) slices

Blend the mango with the lime juice, ginger, and sugar until smooth. Add the fruit juices and rum, and process for a few seconds. Pour over the ice and dress with the fruit.

The Tropical Fruit Punch is simplicity itself and can be varied with different fruit juices. Top with lavish amounts of fruit for a really festive effect and if you want a great long drink, add ginger ale.

Even if you don't celebrate Thanksgiving, and even if you do, this Thanksgiving Special will go down well at any fall or winter party. Be warned, it contains no turkey, pumpkin or succotash.

THANKSGIVING SPECIAL ▲

SERVES 1
2 measures gin
1½ measures apricot brandy
1 measure dry vermouth
½ measure lemon juice

Shake the gin, apricot brandy, dry vermouth, and lemon juice vigorously over ice cubes until well frosted. Strain into a chilled cocktail glass.

COOL YULE MARTINI ▶

A seasonal variation on the classic. Ideal, of course, for serving to guests at a Christmas party.

SERVES 1
3 measures vodka
½ measure dry vermouth
1 teaspoon peppermint schnapps
sprig of fresh mint

Shake the vodka, dry vermouth, and peppermint schnapps over ice cubes until well frosted. Strain into a chilled martini or cocktail glass and garnish with the sprig of fresh mint.

OK CORRAL ◂

SERVES 1

2 measures rye whiskey

1 measure grapefruit juice

1 teaspoon orgeat syrup

Pour the rye whiskey, grapefruit juice, and orgeat syrup over ice cubes and shake vigorously until well frosted. Strain into a chilled cocktail glass.

As long as they are different colors and well chilled, you can use any combination of liqueurs in the Traffic Signal.

TRAFFIC SIGNAL ▸

SERVES 1

crushed ice

½–1 measure mint brandy, chilled

½–1 measure orange brandy, chilled

½–1 measure cherry brandy, chilled

Fill a wine glass or a cocktail glass with crushed ice. Then carefully, in the order listed, pour in the chilled mint, orange, and finally the cherry brandy.

TRETTER'S BAR

PRAGUE

Perverse as it might seem to head for a cocktail bar in a city renowned for its beer, Tretter's in Prague gives Bohemian pubs a run for their money with its much-praised selection of house drinks. Its list of cocktails includes 60 time-honored classics. The remainder are its own creations, devised by its award-winning owner Michael Tretter and his highly trained bar staff.

In appearance, this is an old-school cocktail bar, with a deep red interior, leather loungers, and a long bar. In Prague's Old Town (Stare Mesto) Jewish district, it harks back to the Art Deco period. Yet, despite its own stylish look and a sprinkling of fashionista clientele, it is still remarkably relaxed and laid back. It is true

BEST FOR

house cocktails

JEAN GABIN

During cold winter evenings, Tretter's is fond of serving mulled wine with a twist, adding badian or star anise. This rum-and-brandy-based drink is also a favorite for when the mercury drops.

SERVES 1

3 tablespoons dark rum

3 teaspoons Calvados

1 tablespoon maple or
   almond syrup

⅔ cup hot milk

pinch of nutmeg

Heat the rum, Calvados, and syrup. Fold in the hot milk and pour into a heat-resistant glass. Sprinkle with the nutmeg.

❖

"Bartending is a Tretter family tradition, passed from father to son for 90 years, so it's natural to have a bit of a nostalgic feeling in the bar, evoking 1930s New York or Paris."

Owner, Michael Tretter

it doesn't open its doors to large stag parties, but the policy is otherwise welcoming, egalitarian, and without any dress code.

Small wonder then that the pioneering Tretter's, which started up just as the Czech capital began to emerge as a leading tourist destination, still consistently wins the best cocktail bar award, as voted for annually by readers of the *Prague Post*.

Champagne cocktails always get the thumbs-up here, including Rose's Time made from peach liquor, raspberries, Rose's lime juice, Ciroc vodka, and sparkling wine. Among its popular house cocktails you'll find Thai Parade, a concoction of lychee liqueur, Ciroc vodka, red berry syrup, and lemon juice. Mojitos and Cuba Libres are other solid choices, although Tretter's stands out by often adding ginger, basil, or rosemary. Finally, for those who reckon a visit to Prague just wouldn't be complete without it, Tretter's also serves beer…

TRETTER'S BAR

V Kolkovni 3

110 00 Prague 1

+420 224 811 165

www.tretters.cz

Open daily
7:00 p.m. through 3:00 a.m.

END OF THE EVENING

As the lights dim and the evening finally draws to a close, do you prefer to go out in a blaze of glory with one last blast? Or do you prefer to wind down with a relaxing warm drink that will send you to sleep? Whichever style you favor, you'll find the solution here.

AMARETTO COFFEE ◄

This is a great variation on Irish Coffee. Amaretto is a deliciously sweet, almond-flavored liqueur made from apricot kernels. It is delicious drunk on its own, but also forms the basis for a number of cocktails.

SERVES 1
1 cup hot black coffee
2 tablespoons amaretto
1–2 tablespoons heavy cream

Stir the amaretto into the hot coffee. Then carefully pour the cream on top over the back of a spoon to form a layer.

For once there is a fair degree of agreement about who invented a cocktail and the Irish Coffee is attributed, more or less without dispute, to a chef called Joe Sheridan, who worked at what is now Shannon International Airport in the west of Ireland in the 1940s. One cold, damp evening he apparently decided to cheer up some Americans who'd just arrived by adding Irish whiskey to their coffee. The Americans asked if they were being served Brazilian Coffee, to which Sheridan replied that it was Irish Coffee.

An Amaretto Coffee is usually served in an Irish Coffee glass—a heatproof, short-stemmed glass vessel with a handle, but any heatproof glass will do.

WHITE DIAMOND FRAPPÉ

This is a crazy combination of liqueurs, but it works well once you've added the lemon. Extra crushed ice at the last minute brings out all the separate flavors.

SERVES 1
crushed ice
¼ measure peppermint schnapps
¼ measure white crème de cacao
¼ measure anise liqueur
¼ measure lemon juice

Shake the peppermint schnapps, white crème de cacao, anise liqueur, and lemon juice over some of the crushed ice until frosted. Strain into a chilled cocktail glass and add an extra teaspoonful of crushed ice.

HOT BRANDY CHOCOLATE ▸

Brandy and chocolate certainly have a natural affinity, as this delicious drink demonstrates.

SERVES 4
1 quart milk
4 oz/115 g dark semisweet chocolate, broken
2 tablespoons sugar
5 tablespoons brandy
6 tablespoons whipped cream
grated nutmeg or cocoa powder

Pour the milk into a pan and bring to a boil, then remove from the heat. Add the chocolate and sugar, and stir over a low heat until the chocolate has melted. Pour into four heatproof glasses and then pour the brandy over a spoon onto the top of each one. Finish with a swirl of cream and a sprinkling of nutmeg or cocoa powder.

WHAT ON EARTH? ◂

SERVES 1
2 measures gin
1½ teaspoons powdered (confectioner's) sugar
hot water
twist of lemon peel

Pour the gin into a heatproof glass and stir in the powdered sugar. Fill with hot water and serve with a twist of lemon peel.

RATTLESNAKE ◄

SERVES 1
1 measure Baileys Irish Cream, chilled
1 measure dark crème de cacao, chilled
1 measure Kahlúa, chilled

*Pour the chilled Baileys Irish Cream into a shot glass.
With a steady hand, gently pour in the chilled dark
crème de cacao to make a second layer and then
gently pour in the chilled Kahlúa to make a third layer.
Do not stir.*

HAZY LADY

The bright pink grenadine soon trickles through these
rich nutty-flavored liqueurs to give a pretty base layer.

SERVES 1
½ measure crème de noyaux
½ measure coffee liqueur
½ measure brandy
½ measure orange juice
dash of egg white
dash of grenadine
grated nutmeg

*Shake the crème de noyaux, coffee liqueur, brandy,
orange juice, and egg white together over ice cubes
until frosted. Strain into an iced cocktail glass, and
dress with a dash of grenadine and a sprinkling of
grated nutmeg.*

NAPOLEON'S NIGHTCAP

SERVES 1
1¼ measures cognac
1 measure dark crème de cacao
¼ measure crème de banane
1 tablespoon cream

*Stir the cognac, dark crème de cacao, and crème
de banane together in a mixing glass with ice cubes.
Strain into a chilled cocktail glass and spoon on a layer
of cream.*

Instead of hot chocolate, the small but flamboyant Emperor of France, Napoleon Bonaparte, apparently favored this chocolate-laced brandy with a hint of banana for a nightcap. Daring and extravagant.

IRISH STINGER ▸

SERVES 1
1 measure Baileys Irish Cream
1 measure white crème de menthe

Shake the Baileys Irish Cream and white crème de menthe vigorously over ice cubes until well frosted and strain into a chilled shot or lowball glass.

HEAVENLY ▲

SERVES 1
cracked ice
1½ measures brandy
½ measure cherry brandy
½ measure plum brandy
olives

Put the cracked ice into a mixing glass and pour the brandy, cherry brandy, and plum brandy over it. Stir well to mix and strain into a chilled cocktail glass or brandy snifter. Serve with a couple of olives on a toothpick.

SPOTTED BIKINI

A cute name for an amusing cocktail, but it also tastes great. You may like to add a little sugar to taste.

SERVES 1
2 measures vodka
1 measure white rum
1 measure cold milk
juice of ½ lemon
1 ripe passion fruit
lemon slice

Shake the vodka, white rum, milk, and lemon juice over ice cubes until well frosted. Strain into a chilled medium cocktail glass and add the unstrained passion fruit pulp at the last minute so you can see the black seeds—or spots. Dress with the slice of lemon.

PORT WINE COBBLER ▾

SERVES 1

1 teaspoon superfine sugar

2 measures sparkling water

cracked ice

3 measures ruby port

orange slice

cocktail cherry

Put the sugar into a chilled wine glass and add the sparkling water. Stir until the sugar has dissolved. Fill the glass with cracked ice and pour in the ruby port. Dress with the slice of orange and cocktail cherry.

SPICED HOT CHOCOLATE

This is a treat after an evening spent singing carols on Christmas Eve.

SERVES 4

3¾ cups milk

7 oz/ 200 g good dark chocolate (at least 70% cocoa solids), broken into pieces

2 teaspoons sugar

1 teaspoon allspice

4 sticks cinnamon

2 tablespoons whipped cream

Put the milk, chocolate, sugar, and allspice into a saucepan over a medium heat. Whisk until the mixture is simmering, but not boiling. Remove from the heat and pour into heatproof glasses or mugs with cinnamon sticks and top with a little whipped cream.

PINK ALMOND ▸

SERVES 1

2 measures blended American whiskey

1 measure amaretto

½ measure crème de noyaux

½ measure cherry brandy

1 measure lemon juice

lemon slice

Shake the blended American whiskey, amaretto, crème de noyaux, cherry brandy, and lemon juice vigorously over ice cubes until well frosted. Strain into a chilled goblet and dress with the slice of lemon.

SCOTCH SANGAREE ▸

SERVES 1

1 teaspoon clear honey

sparkling water

cracked ice

2 measures Scotch whisky

spiral of lemon peel

freshly grated nutmeg

Put the honey in a chilled lowball glass with a little sparkling water and stir until dissolved. Add the cracked ice and Scotch whisky, and fill with more sparkling water. Stir gently to mix, then decorate with a spiral of lemon peel and the freshly grated nutmeg.

TIGER'S MILK ◂

SERVES 1
2 measures golden rum
1½ measures brandy
1 teaspoon sugar syrup
⅔ cup milk
crushed ice
ground cinnamon
cinnamon stick

Blend the golden rum, brandy, sugar syrup, and milk with crushed ice until combined. Pour into a chilled wine glass or cocktail glass and sprinkle with the ground cinnamon. Serve with a cinnamon stick.

ALEXANDER

A creamy, chocolate-flavored, gin-based cocktail, decorated with grated nutmeg.

SERVES 1
1 measure gin
1 measure crème de cacao
1 measure light cream
freshly grated nutmeg

Shake the gin, crème de cacao, and light cream vigorously over ice cubes until well frosted. Strain into a chilled cocktail glass and dress with the freshly grated nutmeg.

OLD FASHIONED

This delicious recipe is a perfect illustration of the saying, "Sometimes the old ones are the best."

SERVES 1
1 sugar cube
dash of Angostura bitters
1 teaspoon water
2 measures bourbon or rye whiskey
cracked ice
lemon peel

Place the sugar cube in a small, chilled old-fashioned or lowball glass, then add the dash of Angostura bitters and water. Mash with a spoon until the sugar has dissolved, then pour in the whiskey and stir. Add the cracked ice and decorate with the twist of lemon peel.

BOURBON COBBLER ▸

SERVES 1
1 teaspoon superfine sugar
dash of lemon juice
6 ice cubes, cracked
2 measures bourbon
2 measures Southern Comfort
soda water
peach slice

Put the superfine sugar and lemon juice into a chilled highball glass. Add the cracked ice, bourbon, and Southern Comfort. Fill with soda water and stir to mix. Dress with the slice of peach.

MOONRISE ▴

SERVES 1
1¼ cups medium dry cider
1 tablespoons brown sugar
pinch of ground cinnamon
pinch of freshly grated nutmeg
1 measure apple brandy
2 teaspoons light cream

Put the cider into a saucepan with the brown sugar, pinch of ground cinnamon and pinch of freshly grated nutmeg. Heat gently, stirring until the sugar has dissolved. Pour into a warmed heatproof glass and stir in the apple brandy. Float the light cream on top by pouring gently over the back of a teaspoon.

SALOME

Dark, mysterious, and very risqué—just like the Dance of the Seven Veils.

SERVES 1
⅓ measure gin
⅓ measure Dubonnet
⅓ measure dry vermouth
cherry or pecan nut

Stir the gin, Dubonnet, and dry vermouth together over ice cubes and pour into a chilled cocktail glass, finishing with a cherry or floating pecan nut.

TAMAGOZAKE

This is a brave drink for a special occasion, but be careful not to burn away all the sake. You might want to blow it out before all the flavor and spirit has been burned up.

SERVES 1

1 egg

1 teaspoon sugar

6 measures sake

Beat the egg and sugar together lightly. Boil the sake. Ignite it and then remove from the heat. Stir in the egg-and-sugar mixture and serve in a mug with a handle.

SILVER STREAK

This nightcap can be made with either gin or vodka, but whichever spirit you choose, make sure it is really cold and don't stir—just let the kümmel sink through it.

SERVES 1

4–6 ice cubes, cracked

1 measure gin or vodka, iced

1 measure kümmel, iced

Put the cracked ice in a small old-fashioned or lowball glass and add the gin or vodka. Slowly pour on the kümmel and then drink before the two liquids become too mingled.

HUNGARIAN COFFEE

SERVES 1

2 measures brandy

sugar

strong black coffee, freshly made

1 tablespoons chocolate, grated

whipped cream

cinnamon stick

Put the brandy into a warmed heatproof glass and add sugar to taste. Pour in the coffee and grated chocolate, and stir. When the sugar has completely dissolved and the chocolate has melted, top with the whipped cream and serve with the stick of cinnamon. Don't stir, drink the coffee through the cream.

MOON LANDING ▲

SERVES 1

1 measure vodka

1 measure Tia Maria

1 measure amaretto

1 measure Baileys Irish Cream

Shake the vodka, Tia Maria, amaretto, and Baileys Irish Cream over ice cubes until well frosted. Strain into a chilled shot glass.

KGB ▲

Short for Komityet Gosudarstvyennoi Byezopasnosti, the Soviet Union's notorious intelligence service. Maybe the cocktail was one of the agents' favorite tipples when they fancied a change from vodka.

SERVES 1

1½ measures gin

½ measure kümmel

dash of apricot brandy

Vigorously shake the gin and kümmel over ice cubes with a dash of apricot brandy until well frosted. Strain into a chilled cocktail glass.

PINK SQUIRREL

SERVES 1
cracked ice
2 measures dark crème de cacao
1 measure crème de noyaux
1 measure light cream

*Shake the crème de cacao, crème de noyaux and light
cream vigorously over the cracked ice until well frosted.
Strain into a chilled cocktail glass.*

Crème de noyaux has a
wonderful, slightly bitter,
nutty flavor, but is made from
peach and apricot kernels. It
is usually served as a liqueur,
but combines well with other
ingredients in cocktails, such
as the Pink Squirrel.

WHISKEY RICKEY ▲

SERVES 1
2 measures American blended whiskey
2 measures fresh lime juice
soda water
lime slice

*Half-fill a highball glass with ice and pour in the whiskey
and lime juice. Fill with soda water and dress with the
slice of lime.*

IRISH COW ▾

SERVES 1

1 cup milk

2 measures Irish whiskey

1 teaspoon superfine sugar

Heat the milk in a small saucepan to just below boiling point. Remove from the heat and pour into a warmed heatproof glass or mug. Add the Irish whiskey and superfine sugar, and stir until the sugar has dissolved.

SLOE GIN RICKEY ▸

The original Rickey is made with gin. Here the sloe gin makes it a slightly sweeter, but still sharp and refreshing, drink.

SERVES 1

2 measures sloe gin

2 measures fresh lime juice

soda water

lime slice

Half-fill a highball glass with ice and pour in the sloe gin and lime juice. Fill with soda water and dress with the slice of lime.

WHISKY MAC

This popular classic is enjoyed worldwide as a warming winter drink, so don't be tempted to chill the glass or the drinks.

SERVES 1

1½ measures Scotch whisky

1 measure ginger wine

Carefully pour the Scotch whisky and ginger wine into an old-fashioned glass or lowball glass. Let them mix, but don't stir.

ROADRUNNER ◄

Whether it is named after the real bird or after Wile E. Coyote's nemesis, this is a cocktail for slowing down after a fast-moving day, not for speeding things up.

SERVES 1
1 measure vodka
½ measure Malibu
½ measure amaretto

Shake the vodka, Malibu, and amaretto vigorously over ice cubes until well frosted. Strain into a chilled cocktail glass.

MEXICAN COFFEE

SERVES 1
2 measures Kahlúa
sugar
strong black coffee, freshly made
whipped cream
chocolate, grated

Put the Kahlúa into a warmed heatproof glass and add sugar to taste. Pour in the coffee and stir. When the sugar has completely dissolved, top with the whipped cream and the grated chocolate. Don't stir, just drink the coffee through the cream.

POLISH SIDECAR ◄

SERVES 1
2 measures gin
1 measure blackberry brandy
1 measure lemon juice
fresh blackberry

Vigorously shake the gin, blackberry brandy, and lemon juice over ice cubes until well frosted. Strain into a chilled cocktail glass and decorate with the fresh blackberry.

CSA-BAR

BERLIN

Karl Marx would spin in his grave to see this chic establishment located in the socialist-era boulevard bearing his name. In fact, anyone who knew the once rundown East Berlin district of Friedrichshain in the 1990s would be astounded to see its transformation in the twenty-first century.

Located in the former office of CSA Czech Airlines (from which it takes its name), this sleek minimalist bar has retained the best parts of the original 1950s decor but hasn't been afraid to consign the rest to the garbage can of Cold War history.

Behind the bar counter in the main white room, the back wall boasts curvy backlit elements from the airline's advertising. But the

BEST
Communist conversion

CHARLOTTE COCKTAIL

This cocktail contains a forgotten "old German lady," namely egg liqueur, and is dedicated to another old German lady, the mother of CSA-Bar proprietor René Flatau. Egg liqueur was a favorite tipple of the women of René's mother's generation.

SERVES 1
dash of brown sugar
3 teaspoons egg liqueur
   such as Advocaat
2 tablespoons
   golden rum
2 teaspoons Red Orange
   curaçao
4 tablespoons fresh
   orange juice

Chill a champagne flute or coupette and rim it with the brown sugar by pressing it into a wet paper towel and then dipping it into a saucer of sugar. Shake the egg liqueur, golden rum, curaçao, and orange juice over ice cubes, and double strain the mixture into the glass.

"I wanted to create a timeless style and place. Converting the former CSA airline office into a cocktail bar seemed to be a perfect way of fusing past, present, and future."

Proprietor, René Flatau

bar itself is sleek and modern. The tables in the private "salons" at each end of the bar have built-in spinning ashtrays from the 1960s, but the couches on which guests sit are the very epitome of contemporary elegance. It's all a far cry from the kitschy *Ostalgie* (nostalgia for the former East Germany) one might expect in this neighborhood.

Soft spotlights cast a flattering glow, while tall plate-glass windows overlook the bustling wide street. When it snows—as it does in Berlin in the winter—the scene outside resembles a romantic postcard.

Back inside, there's a long cocktail list to warm you, while jazz and lounge music mellow the mood. Despite the chic surroundings, the atmosphere is very congenial and no critic seems to visit CSA without remarking on the friendly service. Let the staff know your general taste in drinks and they'll produce something just right for you.

CSA-BAR
Karl-Marx-Allee 96,
Friedrichshain
10243 Berlin
Germany
+49 30 290 44 741
www.csa-bar.de

Open daily
8:00 p.m. until the last customer leaves

THE MORNING AFTER

Do you have an urgent need to get back to the land of the living? If you are one of those people who swear by hair of the dog, these tried and trusted recipes will cast out a furry tongue and banish a barking headache. If you are not, you may find it's a question of kill or cure…

PRAIRIE OYSTER ◄   ☆ ▢

This is, without doubt, the ultimate hangover cure. It should be gulped down all at once.

SERVES 1
1 measure brandy
1 teaspoon Worcestershire sauce
2 dashes of Tabasco sauce
salt
freshly ground pepper
1 egg

Shake the brandy, Worcestershire sauce, and Tabasco sauce over ice cubes until well frosted. Add salt and freshly ground pepper to taste, and strain into a chilled old-fashioned glass or lowball glass. Crack the egg into the glass, being careful to avoid breaking the yolk.

In the film *Cabaret,* Sally Bowles, played by Liza Minnelli, makes a Prairie Oyster for her apartment mate Brian Roberts, played by Michael York, although his turns out to have a weird peppermint taste because she's accidentally made it in her toothpaste glass.

It is vital not to scramble the egg yolk and you're supposed to gulp it down all at once, which may be for the best given that some people find a Prairie Oyster somewhat unappealing.

Celery salt and cayenne pepper are additions you can make to a Prairie Oyster. Another twist is the Bloody Prairie Oyster—essentially a Bloody Mary with a raw egg yolk dropped into it.

APPLE RUM RICKEY

SERVES 1
1 measure applejack
½ measure white rum
½ measure lime juice
cracked ice
sparkling water
lime slice

Shake the applejack, white rum, and lime juice vigorously over ice cubes until well frosted. Half-fill a chilled highball glass with the cracked ice and strain the cocktail over it. Fill with the sparkling water and dress with the slice of lime.

BLOODHOUND ▸

This is a rather light, delicate drink—see if you can sniff out the ingredients.

SERVES 1
2 measures gin
1 measure sweet vermouth
1 measure dry vermouth
3 strawberries
crushed ice

Mix the gin, sweet vermouth, dry vermouth, and strawberries in a small blender with a little crushed ice until smooth. Strain into a chilled cocktail glass.

BULLSHOT

This is similar to drinking chilled consommé, but with a kick. It is best drunk really cold.

SERVES 1
1 measure vodka
2 measures beef consommé or homemade broth
dash of fresh lemon juice
2 dashes of Worcestershire sauce
cracked ice
celery salt
lemon peel

Shake the vodka, beef consommé or broth, lemon juice, and Worcestershire sauce vigorously over ice cubes. Put the cracked ice in a cocktail glass and strain the cocktail over it. Sprinkle with the celery salt and garnish with the strip of lemon peel.

PERFECT LOVE

SERVES 1
1 measure vodka
½ measure Parfait Amour
½ measure maraschino liqueur
crushed ice

Shake the vodka, Parfait Amour, and maraschino liqueur together over ice cubes until frosted. Put some crushed ice into a chilled cocktail glass and strain the cocktail over it.

CUPID ▲

SERVES 1
2 measures dry sherry
1 teaspoon sugar syrup
1 egg
dash of Tabasco sauce

Shake the dry sherry, sugar syrup, egg, and dash of Tabasco sauce vigorously over ice cubes until well frosted. Strain into a chilled cocktail glass.

The name of this cocktail is a literal translation of the name of one of its ingredients. Parfait Amour is an unusual purple liqueur flavored with rose petals, almonds, and vanilla.

BROWN COW

If you're not worth a damn 'til you've had your morning coffee, this is a rather good way of taking it.

SERVES 1
cracked ice
1 measure Kahlúa
3 measures milk, chilled

Shake the Kahlúa and chilled milk vigorously over cracked ice until well frosted. Half-fill a chilled lowball glass with cracked ice and strain the cocktail over it.

FERDINAND THE BULL ▲

There isn't any alcohol in this, but it may make you feel bullish nonetheless.

SERVES 1
4 measures tomato juice
4 measures beef broth, chilled
1 measure lime juice
dash of Worcestershire sauce
dash of Tabasco sauce
cracked ice
salt and freshly ground black pepper
lime wedge

Shake all the liquids over ice cubes until well frosted. Half-fill a chilled highball glass with cracked ice and strain the cocktail over it. Season to taste with salt and freshly ground black pepper, and decorate with the lime wedge.

WHITE COSMOPOLITAN

Nothing like its pink cousin, the Cosmopolitan (page 149), this is far more fruity and, instead of vodka, is based on a punchy lemon-flavored liqueur.

SERVES 1
1½ measures Limoncello
½ measure Cointreau
1 measure white cranberry and grape juice
dash of orange bitters
a few red cranberries

Shake the Limoncello, Cointreau, and white cranberry and grape juice together over ice cubes until well frosted. Strain into a chilled cocktail glass, add the dash of orange bitters and decorate with the cranberries.

MINT SUNRISE ‹

SERVES 1
cracked ice
1½ measures Scotch whisky
½ measure brandy
½ measure white curaçao
fresh mint sprig

Pour the Scotch whisky, brandy, and white curaçao over cracked ice in a chilled highball or lowball glass and stir gently. Decorate with the sprig of fresh mint.

Pick-me-ups, such as Widow's Wish, have traditionally included a raw egg as a way of delivering easily digested protein and providing the extra energy needed the day after the night before.

OCEAN BREEZE

This is a breeze to make and as colorful as the foaming ocean on an early morning—just don't dilute it too much.

SERVES 1
1 measure white rum
1 measure amaretto
½ measure blue curaçao
½ measure pineapple juice
club soda

Shake the white rum, amaretto, blue curaçao, and pineapple juice together over ice cubes. Pour into a highball glass and fill with the club soda to taste.

WIDOW'S WISH

SERVES 1
2 measures Benedictine
1 egg
light cream

Shake the Benedictine and the egg vigorously over ice cubes until well frosted. Strain into a chilled lowball glass and fill with the light cream.

SUFFERING FOOL

SERVES 1
1 tablespoon Angostura bitters
cracked ice
2 measures gin
1½ measures brandy
½ measure lime juice
1 teaspoon sugar syrup
ginger beer or ginger ale
cucumber slice
lime slice
fresh mint sprig

Pour the bitters into a chilled highball glass and swirl around. Discard the excess. Half-fill the glass with cracked ice. Pour the gin, brandy, lime juice, and sugar syrup over the ice and stir well. Fill with ginger beer or ginger ale and stir gently. Dress with cucumber, lime, and mint.

NINETEEN PICK-ME-UP ▸

SERVES 1
2 measures Pernod
1 measure gin
¼ teaspoon sugar syrup
dash of Angostura bitters
cracked ice
sparkling water

Shake the Pernod, gin, sugar syrup, and Angostura bitters vigorously over ice cubes until well frosted. Half-fill a highball glass with the cracked ice and strain the cocktail over it. Fill with the sparkling water.

MOONLIGHT

SERVES 1
2 measures applejack
2 measures lemon juice
½ teaspoon sugar syrup
cracked ice

Shake the applejack, lemon juice, and sugar syrup vigorously over ice cubes until well frosted. Half-fill a chilled lowball glass with cracked ice and strain the cocktail over it.

If you're already suffering, the Nineteen Pick-Me-Up could be a cure, but on the other hand it could be the cause of the suffering still to come—you'll have to make up your own mind.

HOT AND DIRTY MARTINI ▲   Y

A Martini, yes, but one that will really put fire in your belly for the day ahead.

SERVES 1
3 measures chili vodka
½ measure dry vermouth
1 teaspoon olive brine
stuffed olive

Shake the chili vodka, dry vermouth, and olive brine over ice cubes until well frosted. Strain into a chilled martini or cocktail glass and garnish with the stuffed olive.

FROZEN PINEAPPLE DAIQUIRI ▲   Y

SERVES 1
crushed ice
2 measures white rum
1 measure lime juice
½ teaspoon pineapple syrup
¼ cup fresh pineapple, finely chopped
pineapple wedges

Mix the crushed ice in a blender with the white rum, lime juice, pineapple syrup, and fresh pineapple until slushy. Pour into a chilled cocktail glass and dress with the wedges of pineapple.

SALTY DOG ☆ 🍸

SERVES 1
1 tablespoon granulated sugar
1 tablespoon coarse salt
lime wedge
6–8 ice cubes, cracked
2 measures vodka
grapefruit juice

Mix the sugar and salt in a saucer. Rub the rim of a chilled highball glass with the lime wedge, then dip it into the sugar-and-salt mixture to frost. Fill the glass with cracked ice and pour the vodka over it. Fill with the grapefruit juice and stir to mix.

PLANTER'S PUNCH REFRESHER ▾ 🍸

SERVES 1
1 measure rum
1 measure lime juice
1–2 teaspoon grenadine
dash of Angostura bitters
cracked ice
club soda or sparkling mineral water

Vigorously shake the rum, lime juice, grenadine, and Angostura bitters over ice cubes until well frosted. Half-fill a chilled highball glass with cracked ice, strain the cocktail over it and fill with the water.

When this cocktail first appeared, gin-based mixes were by far the most popular, but nowadays a Salty Dog is more frequently made with vodka. Choose whichever you prefer, but the two cocktails will taste differently.

GINGER BEER ◄

Yes, it's ginger beer, but not as you normally know it.

SERVES 1
1 cup beer
2 measures ginger brandy

Pour the beer into a chilled beer glass or tankard then add the ginger brandy.

WOO-WOO

SERVES 1
cracked ice
2 measures vodka
2 measures peach schnapps
4 measures cranberry juice

Half-fill a chilled highball glass with cracked ice. Pour the vodka, peach schnapps, and cranberry juice over the ice, and stir well to mix.

MOONSHOT ▲

SERVES 1
cracked ice
dash of Tabasco sauce
2 measures gin
3 measures clam juice
celery stalk

Put some cracked ice into a mixing glass. Splash the Tabasco sauce over the ice and pour in the gin and clam juice. Stir well to mix, then strain into a chilled highball or lowball glass, and dress with the celery.

FUZZY NAVEL

SERVES 1
cracked ice
2 measures vodka
1 measure peach schnapps
1 cup orange juice
Cape gooseberry

Shake the vodka, peach schnapps, and orange juice vigorously over cracked ice until well frosted. Strain into a chilled cocktail glass and decorate with the Cape gooseberry.

The Fuzzy Navel is another one of those cocktails with a name that plays on the ingredients—fuzzy to remind you that it contains peach schnapps and navel because it is mixed with orange juice.

BRANDY COBBLER ▲

SERVES 1
1 teaspoon superfine sugar
3 measures sparkling water
cracked ice
2 measures brandy
lemon slice
cocktail cherry

Put the superfine sugar into a small chilled lowball glass and add the sparkling water. Stir until the sugar has dissolved, then fill the glass with the cracked ice. Add the brandy and stir well. Dress with the slice of lemon and the cocktail cherry.

RUM COBBLER ▸

SERVES 1
1 teaspoon superfine sugar
2 measures sparkling water
cracked ice
2 measures white rum
lime slice
orange slice

Put the superfine sugar into a chilled wine glass. Add the sparkling water and stir until the sugar has dissolved. Fill the glass with the cracked ice and pour in the white rum. Stir well and dress with the slices of lime and orange.

DOG'S NOSE ◂

SERVES 1
1 cup light beer
1 measure gin

Pour the beer into a chilled beer glass or tankard and then add the gin.

RIKKI-TIKKI-TAVI ▶   🍸

SERVES 1
1 sugar cube
dash of Angostura bitters
1 teaspoon brandy
1 teaspoon white curaçao
champagne, chilled

Put the sugar cube into a chilled flute and splash the Angostura bitters over it until it is red but still intact. Pour in the brandy and white curaçao, and fill with the chilled champagne.

YORSH ▲   🍺

SERVES 1
1 cup light beer
2 measures vodka

Pour the beer into a chilled beer glass or tankard and then add the vodka.

Rikki-Tikki-Tavi is a mongoose in a short story of the same name by Rudyard Kipling. Quite what the cocktail has to do with a mongoose is anybody's guess, but the drink will certainly give you a lift.

PACIFIC SUNRISE ◄

SERVES 1

1 measure white tequila
1 measure blue curaçao
1 measure lime juice
dash of bitters

Shake the white tequila, blue curaçao, lime juice, and dash of bitters vigorously over ice cubes until well frosted. Strain into a chilled cocktail glass.

ABSINTHE FRIEND

The original absinthe was a popular cocktail ingredient and digestif, but any pastis, such as Pernod and Ricard, will do just as well instead.

SERVES 1

1 measure gin
1 measure absinthe or Pernod
dash of Angostura bitters
dash of sugar syrup

Shake the gin, absinthe, Angostura bitters, and sugar syrup vigorously over ice cubes until well frosted. Strain into a chilled, lowball glass.

CHAMPAGNE PICK-ME-UP ▲ ☆ ♀ ♀

A glass of this delicious cocktail and you'll be bubbling over with energy.

SERVES 1

2 measures brandy
1 measure orange juice
1 measure lemon juice
dash of grenadine
champagne, chilled

Shake the brandy, orange juice, lemon juice, and a dash of grenadine vigorously over ice cubes until well frosted. Strain the mixture into a wine glass or flute and then fill with the chilled champagne.

WALLIS SIMPSON ▸

SERVES 1

1 measure Southern Comfort

1 teaspoon superfine sugar

dash of Angostura bitters

champagne, chilled

orange slice

Pour the Southern Comfort into a chilled champagne flute, add the superfine sugar, and stir well until dissolved. Add the dash of Angostura bitters and fill with the chilled champagne. Dress with the slice of orange.

STARS AND SWIRLS

You will need a steady hand for this one—preferably two pairs of steady hands.

SERVES 1

1 measure Malibu

large ice cube

½ measure strawberry or raspberry liqueur

1 teaspoon blue curaçao

Chill a small shot glass really well. Pour in the Malibu and add the large ice cube. Carefully pour in the other two liqueurs—the red strawberry or raspberry and the blue curaçao—from opposite sides of the glass. Do this very slowly, so that they slip down the sides of the glass and swirl around.

FROZEN PEACH DAIQUIRI ▸

SERVES 1

crushed ice

2 measures white rum

1 measure lime juice

1 teaspoon sugar syrup

½ peach, peeled, pitted, and chopped

peach slice

Mix the crushed ice in a blender with the white rum, lime juice, sugar syrup, and chopped peach until slushy. Pour into a chilled cocktail glass and dress with the slice of peach.

BLINDING SUNRISE ‹

SERVES 1

1 measure white tequila

1 measure vodka

3 measures orange juice

1 teaspoon triple sec

cracked ice

1 measure grenadine

Shake the white tequila, vodka, orange juice, and triple sec vigorously over ice cubes until well frosted. Half-fill a highball glass with cracked ice and strain the cocktail over it. Slowly pour in the grenadine.

CORPSE REVIVER

After a heavy night, as the name suggests, this cocktail will keep you going and even put you in the mood for another party.

SERVES 1

cracked ice

2 measures brandy

1 measure applejack

1 measure sweet vermouth

Put the cracked ice into a mixing glass. Pour the brandy, applejack, and vermouth over the ice. Stir gently to mix and strain into a chilled cocktail glass.

KAMIKAZE

Drinking this cocktail may be an act of extreme recklessness, but it is so delicious you won't be able to put it down.

SERVES 1

1 measure vodka

1 measure triple sec

½ measure fresh lime juice

½ measure fresh lemon juice

dry white wine, chilled

lime slice

cucumber slice

Shake vodka, triple sec, lime juice, and lemon juice together over ice cubes until well frosted. Strain into a chilled highball glass and fill with the chilled white wine. Dress with the slices of lime and cucumber.

BREAKFAST

It's got the egg, but no bacon—if you've been partying all night and it's now time for breakfast, see if you've got the stomach for this.

SERVES 1

cracked ice

2 measures gin

1 measure grenadine

1 egg yolk

Pour the gin and grenadine over the cracked ice in a shaker and add the egg yolk. Shake vigorously until well frosted and strain into a chilled lowball glass.

PUROBEACH OASIS DEL MAR

PALMA DE MALLORCA

Yoga and massages in the morning and Mojitos and DJs in the evening —that's the beguiling conceptual mix that's made PuroBeach in Mallorca the favorite open-air bar of discerning critics. Luxury guides, such as *Mr. and Mrs. Smith* and *Condé Nast Traveler*, and PuroBeach's well-heeled European customers all agree this man-made peninsula jutting into the Bay of Palma is the coolest beach bar in the Balearics.

The gleaming white complex consists of a revamped Art Deco pavillion and a terraced pool backing right on to the sea. On the pavillion's ground level, there's a restaurant and bar; below them there is a spa with treatment rooms.

BEST
beach bar

ULTRA VIOLET

This extremely popular long drink fits perfectly with the hot summer nights at Puro.

SERVES 1
⅓ cup Absolut Kurant vodka
3 tablespoons blue curaçao
2 teaspoons strawberry syrup
2 teaspoons grenadine
club soda
starfruit (carambola) slices

Shake the vodka, blue curaçao, strawberry syrup, and grenadine together. Half-fill a highball glass with ice cubes then pour the liquid over them. Top up with club soda and garnish with the slices of starfruit (carambola).

❖

"PuroBeach offers well-being in a club environment, so our guests can combine a morning yoga session with the chance to enjoy a chilled Puro Rosé Daiquiri in the evening."

Manager, Peter Estebe

Before sunset, hedonists catch a few rays on the terrace's white sun loungers. Other guests lounge on the restaurant's low white sofas and puff chairs, taking advantage of its wide open porch to enjoy the wonderful views, meanwhile dining on seafood and excellent fusion cuisine.

The interior design has been described as Miami meets Marrakesh and that is certainly true in the bar. Here a large Moroccan shell lamp spans the ceiling and the lampshades are hung with hippie-chic shells.

And it's to the bar—and the terrace—that attention turns for the daily "sunset ceremony." The DJ switches from mellow eclectic and chilled beats to deep house and stylish tracks. Guests switch from smoothies to cocktails. During the beach bar's full-moon parties, celebrity DJs might spin the tunes.

PUROBEACH OASIS DEL MAR
Pagel 1
Cala Estancia
Palma de Mallorca
+34 971 744 744
www.purobeach.com

Open daily
March to October 11.00 a.m.
  to 2.00 a.m.
November to February
Monday to Thursday 11.00 a.m.
  to 7.00 p.m.
Friday to Sunday 11.00 a.m. to 1.00 a.m.

COCKTAIL INDEX

GENERAL INDEX